NO
ORDINARY
JOURNEY

STORIES OF MEN
ON THE OVERLAND TRAILS

MARY BARMEYER O'BRIEN

FARCOUNTRY
PRESS

ISBN: 978-1-56037-838-9

© 2024 by Mary Barmeyer O'Brien
Design by Steph Lehmann

Cover photo: *A long wagon train crossing an arid landscape.*
PHOTOGRAPH BY CHARLES C. PIERCE. PHOTCL PIERCE 07110, C.C. PIERCE COLLECTION OF PHOTOGRAPHS,
THE HUNTINGTON LIBRARY, SAN MARINO, CALIFORNIA.

For more information contact Farcountry Press;
PO Box 5630, Helena, MT 59604; (800) 821-3874; www.farcountrypress.com

CIP information is available from the Library of Congress

Produced and printed in the United States of America

28 27 26 25 24   1 2 3 4 5

For
ERIN TURNER AND MAGGIE PLUMMER,
with deepest thanks;

for my beloved sisters,
BARBARA AND SUSAN;

and for
MAREN, SCOUT, AND NORAH,
who will discover their own remarkable trails

ACKNOWLEDGMENTS

SINCERE THANKS to those who contributed to the successful completion of this book, especially:

- **Erin Turner,** Director of Publications at Farcountry Press, for her steadfast belief in this project and her dedicated help in seeing it through. Much appreciation is also due to her colleagues, the skilled professionals at Farcountry.

- **Maggie Plummer,** loyal friend and fellow writer, for her continual encouragement, proficient editing skills, and careful attention to detail

- **My extraordinary family,** one and all, for their faithful interest in this project, especially:
    - **Dan O'Brien** for providing my author photo and also for offering first-hand details about Steens Mountain and the Malheur National Wildlife Refuge for the story of Benjamin Franklin Owen
    - **Kevin O'Brien** for his covered wagon drawing, which has been used throughout the book
    - **Jenny O'Brien** and Katie O'Brien for their helpful early reading
    - **Steven and Genessa Haber** for providing images from the Pacific Crest Trail near where William Lewis Manly traveled
    - **Barbara Barmeyer and Susan Barmeyer** and the rest of my devoted family and friends for their encouragement and support

- **Angela Claver** and the staff at North Lake County Public Library in Polson, Montana, for assistance with interlibrary loan and other resources

- **Bonnie and Ken Haines** of the Sportsman Lodge in Melrose, Montana, for permission to use their old wagon wheels for photographs

ACKNOWLEDGMENTS

- **The Oregon-California Trails Association** for access to its historical resources and research materials

- **The many** authors, librarians, archivists, mapmakers, photographers, web content writers, historians, and other experts who contributed valuable information about each pioneer selected for this project. Their work has lent detail and clarity to these stories.

- And finally, **the ten pioneer men** who inspired this book by chronicling their extraordinary travels on the overland trails and offering firsthand glimpses into their lives.

CONTENTS

INTRODUCTION

PIONEER MEN TRAVELING THE OVERLAND TRAILS during the mid-nineteenth century found the adventure of their lives—and the most grueling, dangerous endeavor they had ever undertaken.

Most of them were young and looking for a new life. Many were Midwestern farmers who were tired of the never-ending cycle of monotonous chores that left little time for leisure. Malaria lurked in the moist bottomlands where they scratched out their livings, and economic and political conditions had made their lives difficult. Other men had been persecuted, enslaved, or were living in poverty. When they heard stories from the West about rich, free land or California gold nuggets waiting to be claimed, they were eager to go.

Often lacking the know-how needed to complete an overland journey, men set out anyway, planning to learn as they went. Those who brought along their sometimes-reluctant wives and children found out the hard way that traversing the primitive trails with a family was not a simple venture. The trip west was so challenging that no part of it could be considered ordinary. The day-to-day grind of travel wore them down. Deadly cholera struck. Accidents were common. Trailside graves told a grim story. The native peoples populating the route might be friendly trading partners—or dangerous foes who had seen their homelands trampled, depleted, and overtaken.

A few emigrant men turned back in the face of these adversities, but most of them gritted their teeth and pressed on.

They were eager to test their strength against the wild conditions awaiting them. They climbed rock cliffs for the view, forded white-knuckle river currents, shot thundering bison from the backs of farm ponies, and explored snowcapped mountains—the first they had ever seen. They marveled over soda water bubbling straight from the ground, or ice rimming their water buckets in July. All the while, they pushed toward the West, which glowed in their minds like the rising sun.

Many of them, including the men whose stories are retold in this book, chose a covered wagon for transportation. These were generally hardwood farm wagons modified for the journey, although some travelers used ox carts or freight wagons. The strong, boxy body and iron-clad wheels could withstand the beating they had

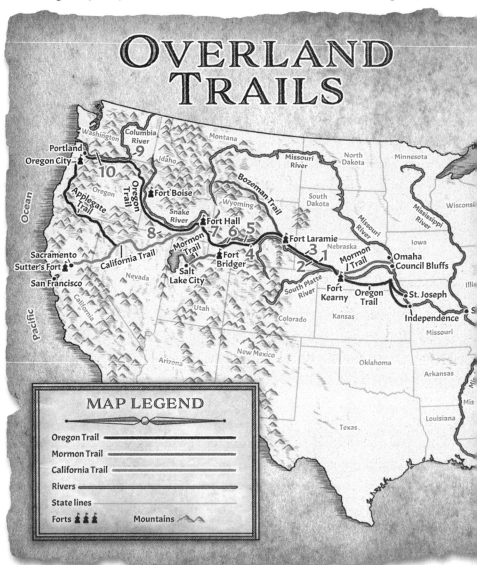

OVERLAND TRAILS

MAP LEGEND

Oregon Trail
Mormon Trail
California Trail
Rivers
State lines
Forts ♟♟♟   Mountains ⌃⌃

to take, and the canvas cover, stretched over arched wooden bows, kept out some of the wind and rain. If the wagon bed, usually about four feet wide, was too crowded for sleeping, the men spread out under it or pitched a tent.

Most of the time, oxen and mules were used to haul the lumbering wagons over the rough trails. Horses were often reserved for riding. Oxen, with their powerful build and brute strength, could pull the heaviest loads. Mules were faster, but more expensive to use. Whichever was chosen, the animals' staying power and health were critical to a successful overland journey. Most men paid close attention to their condition and went far out of their way to find feed and water for them. Sometimes, however, thousands of cattle had already grazed the trail ahead, and there were plenty of long, arid stretches to cross. Finding good forage, or even water, was often impossible.

Covered wagon travel had its drawbacks. The unwieldy conveyances were slow and heavy. On a good day, emigrants could travel only about twenty or twenty-five miles. The wagons mired in mud, jolted hard over rocks, and were swept away down rushing rivers. Axles and wagon tongues broke. Wheels cracked apart. Offering scant protection from the elements, the wagons occasionally tipped over in violent windstorms or on steep slopes. Their 2000-pound weight, frequently loaded with 2500 pounds of supplies and provisions, exhausted the animals pulling them. At times, travelers had to unload their belongings so the oxen or mules could manage a steep uphill haul, lugging the heavy

LANDMARK LEGEND

1. Courthouse Rock	6. South Pass
2. Chimney Rock	7. Soda Springs
3. Scotts Bluff	8. City of Rocks
4. Independence Rock	9. The Whitman Mission
5. Devil's Gate	10. The Dalles

items to the top themselves. On downslopes, wagons required primitive brakes, ropes, and physical strength from both men and animals to prevent them from careening wildly to the bottom.

Still, westward-bound emigrants considered them the best option, especially men with wives or families, and those hauling supplies to the new land. Travelers almost always joined with others, forming large wagon trains for support and safety. Later in the trip, these typically splintered into smaller fragments as disagreements escalated.

The 2000-mile-long roads they traversed were little more than rude trails stretching from the Missouri River nearly to the Pacific Ocean. Early pioneers encountered boulders, mud, dense timber, thick undergrowth, and rushing waterways. Later travelers, following imprecise guidebooks, were still hampered by the harsh landscape, but were also beset by problems left behind by earlier overlanders: choking dust or deep mud from heavily trampled ground, disease from polluted water, native peoples alarmed and angered over the flood of emigrants rushing onto their lands, and the terrible stench of dead stock animals left to rot. Every route was littered with discarded belongings.

A journey west required careful planning. Most wagons were laden with cooking gear, bedding, household goods, clothing, tools, and enough food to last four to six months. Staples included beans, bacon, flour (200 pounds for each adult), rice, cornmeal, sugar, dried fruit, and coffee. Some pioneers brought along vinegar, tea, or whiskey, partly for their medicinal value. Unpopular hardtack (dense, dry biscuits made from flour, water, and salt) was sometimes used when weather conditions prevented emigrants from cooking or when there was no fuel for a campfire.

Many men of the era were inexperienced at preparing meals or washing clothes. They found themselves learning by trial and error as they mended their own shirts or washed laundry in streams. Cooking over a fire proved especially challenging. They burned bacon, spilled food from their cookpots into the flames, and made biscuits that refused to rise. But it didn't take long to perfect charbroiling wild game or making hot coffee with flapjacks.

An overwhelming proportion of overland travelers were men, especially during the California Gold Rush of 1849. These men were a product of their era, upbringing, and the ethics of their society. Time and time again, the trails brought out the best in them. Some sacrificed their own safety and comfort for the benefit of others, treating their families, companions, and animals with kindness and respect. Others honored and admired the native peoples they encountered and revered the natural world around them. Sharing their limited, irreplaceable provisions was common. Some even died offering a helping hand.

For others, though, overland travel brought out their shortcomings. Many failed to consider the plight of the native peoples they killed and displaced. Some had a thoughtless disregard for the natural world, as they trampled, littered, and overgrazed every route west. Others seemed indifferent to the severe suffering of the work animals that made the journey possible. Men often overlooked the vital contributions of the women traveling with them, who performed fully half of the trip's exhausting tasks. Worn down by the daily grind, emigrants became irritable and impatient. Whiskey-fueled fights erupted, and trouble brewed.

Still, they pressed on.

A small percentage of pioneer men kept diaries or other written records, defying the fatigue that dogged them to write about each day's events. Some jotted down simple notations about the weather or the availability of grass and water for the animals. Others filled their journals with meticulous descriptions, humor, philosophical musings, and personal revelations. Sometimes, they wrote down a detail so striking it stands out more than a century and a half later: a life-saving spring in the desert, the death of a loved one, an unimaginable accident, or the pure glory of the West's dramatic landscape.

Without these colorful diaries, memoirs, and autobiographies, men's stories of their overland journeys would have vanished into the past. Those who contributed written accounts left a rich legacy, providing firsthand glimpses into their lives. Offering windows into the past, these pioneers chronicled their journeys with candor and personality.

The ten men whose stories are retold in this book represent a small cross section of covered wagon men who made the long, strenuous journey to the West. Dr. John Hudson Wayman practiced medicine on the trail. Artist James F. Wilkins's sole purpose was to sketch the overland route to create a larger work of art when he returned home. William Swain, who deeply loved his wife and family, undertook the trip to the California goldfields to give them a chance at a better future. Alvin Aaron Coffey was enslaved; he went west seeking freedom for himself and his family. Others were drawn to the trails by the promise of religious tolerance or a healthier climate.

Their stories, like their lives, are diverse and unique. These resourceful, courageous men overcame long odds and desperate hardships to forge new lives for themselves, their friends, and their families.

ROUGH ROAD
TO OREGON COUNTRY

The Story of William T. Newby

EVENING HAD FALLEN when William T. Newby climbed a low hill to survey the glassy Kaw River ahead. His work for the day was done, although Sarah Jane, his nineteen-year-old wife, was still cleaning up after supper. It was 1843, and they were finally starting out on the Oregon Trail, after months of preparation. He was sure that this trip across the continent would bring them health and prosperity, if only they could get through to the legendary Willamette Valley. There, according to word of mouth, beautiful rich farmland, a gentle climate, and a chance to start afresh awaited them.

The company had been on the trail only a few days, but already it was late May. They'd gathered with the other members of their large group near today's Kansas City, forming the first major wagon train to undertake the long journey to Oregon country. William and Sarah Jane McGary Newby were among about 1,000 travelers, some of whom were on foot or horseback. Tomorrow, they would cross the Kaw (Kansas) River.

Newby turned his gaze to the ungainly train of about 120 wagons, circled for the night. Already he had heard grumbling from those who wanted to split up. Those driving cattle should be in one group, they felt, and those who weren't should make up a second lighter company. He agreed that the large number of animals was unwieldy. There were several thousand of the milling, balky creatures following the wagons, challenging the drovers to keep them together.

The cumbersome group forded the Kaw, a six-day undertaking. Soon after that, near the Big Blue River in today's state of Kansas, the train split up. The two

1

companies would travel in close proximity for mutual protection, but those without extra cattle could move more freely. The Newbys were with the "cow column," as the group with livestock was called, indicating that they must have had spare oxen along.

Newby, twenty-three, briefly recorded each day's travel in a small, lined notebook. Written mostly in ink, his journal survives to this day—water stained and

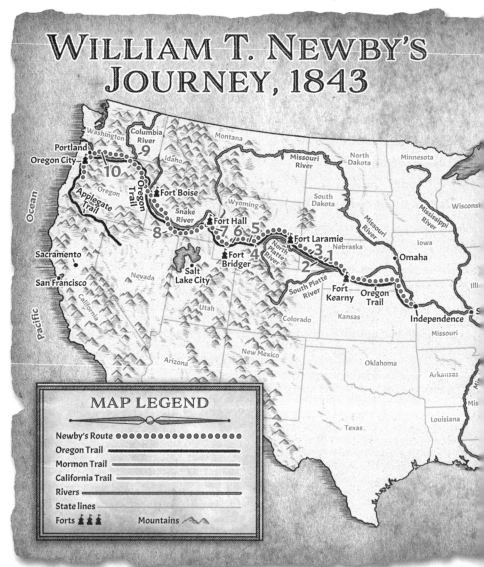

WILLIAM T. NEWBY'S JOURNEY, 1843

MAP LEGEND

Newby's Route ●●●●●●●●●●●●●●●●●●
Oregon Trail ——————
Mormon Trail ——————
California Trail ——————
Rivers ——————
State lines ————
Forts ♟♟♟   Mountains ⌃⌃⌃

worn, but still readable. Many of his entries were brief, listing the number of miles traveled, what the weather was like, and one or two other details. Interestingly, Newby didn't mention his wife in his trail journal.

Both of his parents had died when he was a small child, and his youth had been a struggle during which he received little education. Some sources say he had less than six months of schooling. In that short time, however, he learned to read and write.

"Reached the buffilow grass & had a verry stormmey night," he wrote on June 21.

Spring storms were common on the rolling plains, and the cow column encountered more than one. The wind was so wild that the men had to hold their wagons down to keep them from blowing over, and the sleeping tents were nearly carried away. Still, the group made decent time heading northwest on the primitive road as it dipped into muddy hollows, crossed streams, skirted ponds, and finally reached the turbid Platte River, which they followed through present-day Nebraska. Dr. Marcus Whitman, who had left his mission settlement on the Columbia Plateau to spend the winter in the Midwest, joined them as a physician and guide.

No doubt the Newbys learned much about wagon travel during their first month. Baking bread and roasting antelope meat over buffalo chip campfires were almost certainly among Sarah Jane's many tasks, while William concentrated his efforts on caring for the livestock. He also wrote about hunting buffalo. Early in the trip, before

LANDMARK LEGEND

1. Courthouse Rock
2. Chimney Rock
3. Scotts Bluff
4. Independence Rock
5. Devil's Gate
6. South Pass
7. Soda Springs
8. City of Rocks
9. The Whitman Mission
10. The Dalles

they grew too weary, the Newbys may have socialized around a campfire in the evenings. Perhaps they danced under the stars to the tune of someone's fiddle. Undoubtedly, they made new friends.

On July 3, the travelers crossed the South Platte River in today's state of Nebraska, a daunting task due to spring runoff. Even a somewhat shallow stream could sweep away wagons, household goods, animals, and people, and Newby volunteered to help find the best route. Fording was slow, but finally the company got the wagons across, landing two and a quarter miles downstream. Newby noted that he waded and swam the river seven times during the operation. There was no mention of celebrating the Fourth of July; the formidable crossing had fatigued everyone. That night they camped without firewood.

The Oregon Trail followed unique landmarks scattered along its 2,000-mile length. Courthouse Rock, Chimney Rock, and Scotts Bluff were natural wonders that the emigrants noted in awe as they neared present-day Wyoming. Many carved their initials in the rock features or wrote their names in axle grease on the stony surfaces. Some climbed the precipices looking for vistas and adventure.

On July 12, Newby's party reached Fort Laramie in today's southeastern Wyoming. His diary didn't mention stopping, but most travelers used the fort to rest, restock their supplies, and repair their wagons. Established in 1834, the rough outpost was considered an island of civilization in a vast sea of wilderness. If the group did stop, it was only briefly. The next day, Newby wrote that they had moved on to a new river crossing.

It was beyond Fort Laramie where the party experienced its first death. A six-year-old boy, Joel Hembree, slipped from his parents' wagon tongue and was run over by the heavy, iron-clad wheels, causing massive injuries. The boy died the next day and was buried on the prairie while his weeping parents looked on. It is thought that Newby chiseled the youngster's headstone—a large, flat-sided boulder into which he etched the boy's name and the year. Today the stone can still be seen; it is the oldest identified grave along the Oregon Trail.

By then, the Newbys were aware that river crossings were harrowing and dangerous, but they still were unprepared for what happened while fording the North Platte in present-day southeast Wyoming. Their wagon, which was tied to another for security, came untethered. In the swift current, it tumbled over and over as it was carried downstream. Newby and two companions swam behind and *"follerd after it a bout one mile"* nearly drowning in the process. The men struggled ashore and eventually found the battered wagon three miles downriver. They were able to retrieve it without more damage, but the Newbys had lost their gun, ox yoke, ax, and a bucket of tar and grease used to lubricate the wheels.

On July 28, the wagon train reached Independence Rock, a 1,900-foot-long granite dome that rose dramatically from the flatlands. Newby etched his name into the hard surface.

As the miles dragged on, the wagons began to break down. Somewhere in today's state of Wyoming, fellow traveler Jesse Applegate turned his wagon into a two-wheeled cart when an axle broke and there was no timber to replace it. Others had trouble when the arid western air dried out their wooden wheels, causing them to shrink away from the iron rims. Soaking the wheels in a stream overnight helped prevent the rims from slipping off.

The emigrants gained altitude and began seeing snow as they edged around the craggy Wind River Range, an impressive new sight for travelers from the flat Midwest. Crossing the Continental Divide at beautiful South Pass, Newby noted its gradual ascent and descent, an observation made by many pioneers. Some hardly realized they had reached an important milestone. They were finally at their journey's halfway point, having come nearly 1,000 miles. At nearly 7,500 feet of elevation, nights were cold.

Enthusiasm had worn off. The days were monotonous and exhausting. Even small disagreements could turn serious, and irritation ran high. Two men in nearby companies died. A child was born. Newby's journal gave few details. The group pressed on to the Green River and then traversed the long stretch to Fort Bridger, a fur-trading outpost established in 1843 in today's southwest Wyoming. As the party lay over for a day, a little girl died and was buried near the fort. It was August 15.

Traveling fourteen to twenty miles each day, the company continued to push westward, hoping to avoid more of the deaths that had begun to plague them. The Newbys were probably among those who comforted the survivors. Overland travelers grew close through shared experiences and the need for support, and the bonds often lasted a lifetime.

Trading for horses and other items with the indigenous Snake people, the group left Wyoming and entered the southeast corner of present-day Idaho. Mountainous terrain near the Bear River slowed their travel, but they kept a fairly steady pace until they reached another long-awaited landmark: Soda Springs. Newby, like the others, was fascinated by the effervescent water that bubbled from the earth there. He took a drink, noting that it tasted *"like sody,"* and tested its temperature. Steam shot from holes in the ground.

The group pressed on to Fort Hall near today's city of Pocatello, Idaho. Established in 1834 as a trading post, the fort was located in the Snake River valley. Newby reported that the wagon train stopped for a day. Marcus Whitman left the group on horseback for his mission at Waiilatpu near present-day Walla Walla, Washington. He had established the operation in 1836 with his wife, Narcissa Prentiss Whitman. Inviting the emigrants to detour to the small settlement later in the trip, he promised to resupply them.

The travelers knew they would soon have to cross the treacherous Snake River, one of the journey's most difficult passages. After dealing with another man's death from illness, Newby's company chose a place far south of the fort where the steep bluffs weren't too high and islands divided the river into manageable sections. It was September 11. They crossed each channel, hitching the wagons together in groups to attempt the final stretch where the water was swift and deep. The river rose high on the wagon beds, but the crossing was made without major mishap.

Heading toward Fort Boise, Newby mentioned the search for water and grass almost daily in his journal. Finding both was difficult on this dry section of the trail, and the animals were worn out. He indicated his relief that the tough sagebrush underfoot was thinning out. They crossed the Boise River and stopped near the fort on the modern-day border of Idaho and Oregon. The trail worsened after it traversed the Snake again and led them into the Blue Mountains. Newby wrote that the wagons inched over the rough road, fording streams and lumbering up steep slopes, where they encountered snow. Dense timber blocked the way. By then, it was early October.

The pioneers went out of their way to stop at the Whitman mission. Marcus Whitman had been called away before the wagon train arrived, but he had instructed a man in charge to trade with the emigrants, so they were able to get the pork, beef, flour, and potatoes they needed. Newby was disappointed by the high prices they had to pay, but they made their purchases and moved on to the Hudson's Bay Company's Fort Walla Walla, about twenty-five miles to the west.

On October 18, the Newbys and some of the other wagon travelers acquired canoes, made arrangements for their oxen and other belongings, and said goodbye to their company. They would paddle down the Columbia River for the last 250 miles to Fort Vancouver, the end of the overland journey.

The canoeists set out the next day, navigating the great waterway with the help of local native guides. The trip began ominously for the Newbys and another traveler who were sharing a boat. As they navigated some rapids, the small craft hit a submerged rock and *"stove up,"* as Newby put it. The three were dumped into the strong current. Accounts differ about whether the canoe filled with water or was snatched away, but the boaters had to climb onto a large boulder. They clung there, shivering and desperately trying not to lose their grip as the cold water rushed around them.

William T. Newby made the long journey to Oregon's Willamette Valley as part of the Great Migration of 1843. He platted the town of McMinnville, Oregon, which he named after his hometown of McMinnville, Tennessee. PHOTOGRAPH COURTESY OF THE OREGON HISTORICAL SOCIETY, CARTES-DE-VISITE COLLECTION; ORG. LOT 500; B5.F798-3; ORHI66491.

Their guide, skilled at navigating the mighty Columbia, found the canoe and took them ashore to warm up by a campfire. The Newbys and the others in their party were able to resume the hazardous journey the following day. But the October weather, with its strong, cold headwinds, delayed them time after time. Chilled, wet, and exhausted, the group portaged some areas and inched their way downriver, hiring native canoeists to run the small crafts through the dangerous rapids at The Dalles. Eventually they made their way to Cascade Falls (about forty miles east of today's Portland, Oregon, now submerged under waters controlled by Bonneville Dam). A boat met them there. It had been dispatched by Dr. John McLoughlin, the chief factor of Fort Vancouver, who had heard of their plight. Grateful for McLoughlin's generous assistance, the emigrants huddled aboard the vessel in the cold November rain and were taken to the fort.

After resting, they were transported about twenty miles farther to Willamette Falls and Oregon City on the Willamette River. McLoughlin, who was known for his kind hospitality, also facilitated this last leg of the trip.

Newby's account of his journey ended there with an entry dated November 6, 1843.

Arriving in the Willamette Valley was just the beginning for William and Sarah Jane Newby. In the years that followed, they took up a donation land claim in the beautiful green hills southwest of present-day Portland. Their home was in the heart of the new Yamhill County, known for its dark, rich soil and mild climate. Newby built a gristmill between Baker and Cozine Creeks and a store on the site of present-day McMinnville, which he laid out and named after his birthplace in Tennessee.

The Newbys had at least eight children and are thought to have built a distinguished home in McMinnville. In the late 1850s they donated a portion of their land for a college, which today has become the well-known Linfield University. A small dorm on campus is named Newby Hall. Newby Elementary School is nearby.

William Newby also served as a state senator in 1870. He died at the age of sixty-four in McMinnville in 1884; Sarah Jane followed in 1887.

Memories of their early trip across the continent remained with them all their lives. Among the first to travel the Oregon Trail in covered wagons, the couple overcame a dangerous route filled with enormous obstacles. Their overland journey enabled them to create a new life for themselves and their soon-to-be family in the faraway land that had beckoned to them.

William T. Newby's trail diary illustrates much about the man who wrote it. Loyal to his task, he made use of rare quiet moments to record his westward journey. His plain words provide hints about his views, while illustrating the customs and behavior of 1840s pioneers. He offers clues to his temperament by reporting life-changing events with unruffled practicality. Newby also created a valuable historical record of the early Oregon Trail. The successful completion of the hazardous trip was a highpoint of his life—and the beginning of the ambitious endeavors that marked the remainder of his years.

TRAPPED IN MOUNTAIN SNOW

The Story of Patrick Breen

THE TRIP WEST SEEMED PROMISING AT FIRST. In 1846, Patrick Breen and his wife Margaret (Peggy) left their home in the Territory of Iowa with their seven children, three covered wagons, plenty of oxen, and ample supplies for the long trip to California. They started along the overland trail in mid-May, joining the now-famous Donner party near Independence, Missouri. Their companions seemed prepared and capable, and the route was distinct, if not yet well traveled. They'd gotten a late start, but no one was concerned.

There are many, varied historical accounts of the ill-fated trip, but Patrick Breen wrote a partial firsthand report in his terse diary. He chronicled the deadly months later in the journey when his family and their fellow travelers were trapped for the winter in the snowbound Sierra Nevada.

At first, the group was made up of about a dozen families and a handful of single men. Roughly half were children. Among the party was the fatherly George Donner, a Midwestern

Patrick Breen's westward journey with the ill-fated Donner Party was one of the most harrowing in wagon train history.
OVAL PORTRAIT OF PATRICK BREEN, SR., CALIFORNIA FACES: SELECTIONS FROM THE BANCROFT LIBRARY PORTRAIT COLLECTION, POR: BREEN, PATRICK, THE BANCROFT LIBRARY, UNIVERSITY OF CALIFORNIA, BERKELEY.

farmer in his early sixties, his wife Tamsen, who had been a schoolteacher, and their five daughters. George's brother Jacob, his spouse Elizabeth, and their seven children joined them. So did businessman James Reed, his wife Margaret, and their four young ones. Although generally prosperous and well-stocked, the travelers were inexperienced in overland travel and had little frontier savvy. But they had planned well and felt confident in their ability to make the trip.

As the wagons began to roll west, Patrick Breen may have taken quiet stock of his own family. Slight, dark-haired Peggy was forty years old, compared to his fifty-one. She would be a stalwart partner on this dangerous and uncertain journey. Their children—a passel of boys (John, fourteen; Edward, thirteen; Patrick, nine; Simon, eight; James, five; and Peter, three) and one infant daughter, Isabella— were ready to undertake the trip. The Breens were accompanied by their cheerful Irish friend and neighbor, Patrick Dolan. Some historians believe the Breens were searching for a place with rich farmland, a pleasant climate, and greater tolerance for their devout Catholicism.

Both had emigrated from Ireland and settled in Canada. Patrick arrived there in 1828 and Peggy came at an unknown date. They married and began their family. After a few years, they moved to the United States. But Anti-Catholicism had taken hold, and the Breens may have thought that California, with its history of Franciscan missions, was the answer to their prayers.

Perhaps Breen breathed a sigh of anticipation as he guided his wagons along the wide, silvery Platte River, heading westward. As the spring sunshine warmed his face and bright wildflowers punctuated the green prairie, he may have jiggled little Isabella or Peter on his knee as he drove, while Peggy joined the older children walking. He almost certainly cast a careful eye on his oxen, watching for any sign of weakness or a limp. When violent prairie thunderstorms whipped across the plains, he and Peggy would have secured the shivering children in the one wagon that wasn't full of supplies and provisions.

But Breen's diary didn't mention these things; he didn't begin writing it until his family reached the Sierra Nevada near the end of the trip. Other members of the Donner party recorded the first part of the journey.

The road along the Platte was relatively easy. Thirteen-year-old Virginia Reed wrote that at the end of each day, the wagons formed a circle to create an inner corral for the livestock. The wagon train's hunters supplied the hungry travelers with buffalo or antelope meat, which sizzled over their fires. Later, some of the group would gather around a campfire for socializing and singing.

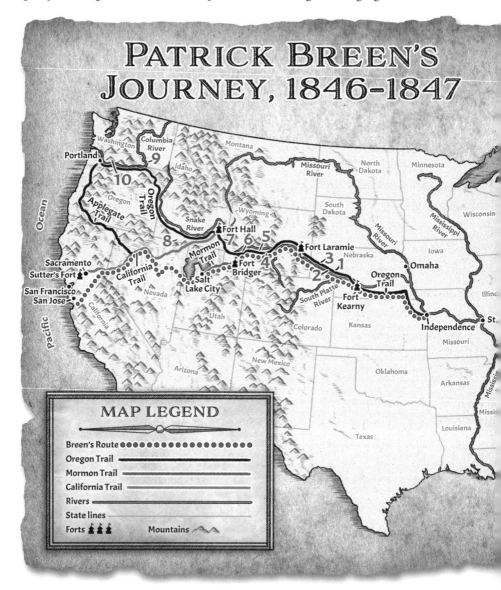

They celebrated the Fourth of July at Fort Laramie with an elaborate dinner, brandy, music, and a salute of guns. After a two-day rest, they were back on the trail, marveling at the number of Sioux who rode past as the party pushed toward the Sweetwater River. They passed Independence Rock and Devil's Gate—a deep, scenic gorge cut by the Sweetwater—and easily crossed the Continental Divide at South Pass. As with many wagon parties, their numbers flexed and grew as they traveled.

Despite the loss of several oxen in the drylands, the party made it safely to Fort Bridger. There they made a deadly mistake. After much debate, some of the travelers decided to take the new Hastings Cutoff, which broke away from the main California Trail, entered today's state of Utah, and passed to the south of the Great Salt Lake. It was said to reduce the distance to the Humboldt River by three hundred miles, and was touted as the better course. Cut-offs were tempting to the pioneers as they pushed westward. These rough shortcuts promised to save time and miles, but were often harsher and poorly mapped.

Since it was already the end of July, about ninety travelers—including the Breens, Donners, and Reeds—took the cutoff. In the Wasatch Mountains east of the Great Salt Lake, the party and their twenty or so wagons encountered rugged terrain with no apparent road. They had to cut trees, heave boulders aside, and hack their way through impenetrable undergrowth. Progress slowed

LANDMARK LEGEND

1. Courthouse Rock
2. Chimney Rock
3. Scotts Bluff
4. Independence Rock
5. Devil's Gate
6. South Pass
7. Soda Springs
8. City of Rocks
9. The Whitman Mission
10. The Dalles

to barely a crawl. Accounts differ as to how long the group was delayed, but many believe it was as much as two or three weeks.

When they finally emerged onto the plains, the travelers were worn out, discouraged, and dreadfully behind schedule. Knowing that time was short, they tried to hurry across the unforgiving salt flats and desert, but the punishing landscape took its toll. They lost time as well as a substantial number of cattle and wagons. Provisions were getting so low that George Donner, now captain of the group, asked for volunteers to hurry ahead to Sutter's Fort (today's city of Sacramento) for supplies. Two men, Charles Stanton and William McCutchen, offered to go.

After another two hundred miles of grueling travel, the Donner party skirted the Ruby Mountains in present-day northeastern Nevada. Just beyond, the Hastings Cutoff finally rejoined the main California Trail. The so-called shortcut had actually added distance to the route. By then, it was the end of August. Ahead lay the long trek down the Humboldt River, the harsh Forty Mile Desert, and the Sierra Nevada, where the mountain passes and canyons were known to be steep and perilous. As moods continued to plummet, the group moved ahead.

The sluggish, snakelike Humboldt, meandering approximately three hundred miles across the Nevada deserts, led the pioneers toward California. Travelers found this hot, treeless stretch of the journey tedious and hard to endure, often writing of the river's foul water, muddy sloughs, and biting insects. It did, however, provide daily water for the livestock before finally seeping underground near the Forty Mile Desert in today's western Nevada.

Patrick and Peggy Breen might have suspected that there would be trouble among the emigrants as exhaustion set in. But it was a shock when James Reed fatally stabbed one of the teamsters, possibly in self-defense, along the Humboldt. Reed was banished and sent ahead alone. The Breens undoubtedly tried to shield their children from the violence, but the incident caused morale to sink even lower.

The wagon train's desolate trip down the Humboldt dragged on. Oxen continued to fail and were left behind. Nearly forty of the cattle were killed or driven off by Paiutes seeking to halt this invasion into their homelands. By the time the travelers reached the river's end at the Humboldt Sink and began crossing the Forty Mile Desert, it was mid-October, dangerously late in the season. Everyone was on foot to spare the remaining oxen their weight in the wagons. After a desperate push across the arid miles, the party finally reached the beautiful Truckee River. There, amid lush cottonwood trees, most of them paused for several days to rest and wait for Stanton and McCutchen to return.

True to his promise, Charles Stanton showed up leading several loaded mules. William McCutchen had fallen ill in California, but Stanton had followed through with the help of two Miwok guides. He told the group that he had seen James Reed approaching the settlements, emaciated, but alive.

The party pressed on as rain began to fall. In the Sierra Nevada foothills, as they started up the mountain pass, the cold drizzle turned to snow. Stanton went ahead to assess the situation. When he returned, he urged the group to make an immediate push to the summit, by then within reach. But the travelers, too depleted, decided to spend the night on the eastern slope of the mountains and climb the few miles to the summit in the morning.

That night, heavy snow continued to fall. In the morning, all attempts to reach the top failed. The weary travelers returned to Truckee Lake (now called Donner Lake) in present-day northeast California, realizing they were trapped. The Donner brothers, who had been bringing up the rear, were stranded six or seven miles farther back on Alder Creek. It was the end of October, and after traveling nearly 2,000 miles, the group was stalled roughly one hundred miles from the settlements.

What went through Patrick Breen's mind that fateful day? He and Peggy had nine mouths to feed, and few provisions left. As the canvas wagon covers sagged under the weight of the snow, temperatures dropped. Their remaining oxen, gaunt and tired out, could barely flounder among the drifts. Inside the first wagon, the Breens' younger children almost certainly shivered and cried as the freezing wind blew through their inadequate clothing. Looking around, Breen could see nothing but a vast, white wilderness dotted with snow-covered pine and fir. The mountain summits and the elusive pass seemed far away. Game animals had already fled to the lower valleys.

DONNER LAKE.

126. Donner Lake and Eastern Summit,
from top of Summit Tunnel, western Summit.

This 1860s photograph shows Donner Lake, where Patrick Breen and his family, along with others of the Donner Party, were stranded during the winter of 1846-47. COURTESY OF DEPARTMENT OF SPECIAL COLLECTIONS, STANFORD UNIVERSITY LIBRARIES.

One thing stayed strong: the Breens' faith in God. It must have seemed like a miracle when a small, crudely constructed log shack appeared among the trees. It had been built by an earlier emigrant party. Historians believe it was about fourteen feet long by twelve feet wide, made of pine sapling poles, and roofed with brush and animal hides. There was an opening large enough for a person to enter; it also let in the only light. A rough chimney and stone hearth stood at one end. Breen immediately settled his family into it, along with their friend Patrick Dolan.

Others in the party quickly constructed two more shacks and built a makeshift lean-to along an outer wall of Breen's cabin. Back at Alder Creek, the Donners hurriedly made primitive shelters using brush and possibly their canvas wagon covers. Some historians believe they used quilts and clothing and, later, animal hides to cover the crude dwellings.

With his family shielded from the wind and snow, Breen probably sank to his knees and thanked God for the shack, even though it was leaky, cold, dark, and cramped. It was hardly big enough for three or four people; with more, it was unbearably small. They would make the most of it. Peggy Breen, too, was determined to care for her family.

They killed one of the cattle, built a fire, cooked some of the meat, and ate sparingly. Lugging quilts from the wagons, they made makeshift beds on the frozen dirt floor, crowded into every inch of space. Perhaps the older children took turns warming Baby Isabella under their clothing as their mother worked. The snow continued to fall, piling into drifts and blowing through the cabin's cracks.

On November 20, Breen started his diary. Finding several sheets of paper that had survived the journey, he folded and trimmed them into a small thirty-two-page booklet. Then he recorded his thoughts, one day at a time. Wedged into a dark corner of the crowded shanty, he probably wrote by firelight or daylight coming through the crevices. His entries were sometimes fervent pleas to his Heavenly Father. He jotted down observations about the weather and the most urgent happenings. Again and again, he mentioned how difficult it was to get firewood, which they needed for survival. His words were simple, matter of fact, and impassive. He understated the dire circumstances around him, and there was little mention of his family. Nonetheless, he managed to convey powerfully the horror of the party's experience during that menacing winter.

The snow kept coming.

On November 24, he wrote: *". . . killed my last oxen today will skin them tomorrow . . ."*

Less than a week later, he noted: *". . . snow about 5 1/2 feet or 6 deep difficult to get wood . . ."*

The annexed Diary
was Kept by Patrick Breen.
who with his family Viz
Patrick Breen, Margret Breen,
John Breen, Edward Breen,
Patrick Breen jr, Simon Breen.
James Breen, Peter Breen.
Isabella Breen, —— were
a part of what is Called the
"Donner Party" that was
detained by Snow on the
Sirrea Nevada. the winter
of 1846–'47 an account of
their Sufferings was published
by me in the "California
Star" May 22d 1847.
I am told Mr Breen,
in a family are at San
Juan, Monterey County
Cald Mr Breen.

Meanwhile, James Reed fretted as he waited for his wife and children to meet him at Sutter's Fort. Not knowing what had happened to them but fearing the worst, he organized a rescue. In spite of gathering horses, provisions, and the company of William McCutchen, he was forced to turn back when the route to Truckee Lake was far too buried in snow for passage. Reed vowed to try again.

At Truckee Lake, the days dragged on. Breen must have thought all of them were doomed. Food, already scarce, was dwindling. Efforts at hunting and fishing failed miserably. Attempts to cross the summit were met with exhaustion and bitter disappointment. In mid-December, about seventeen of the strongest men, women, and older children decided to hike to the settlements to get help, an expedition now known to historians as the Forlorn Hope. They set out with the barest provisions and homemade snowshoes, thinking they could reach the valleys in about ten days. Under fierce conditions and unsure of the route, they traveled slowly and ran out of food. As the trip dragged on, more than half of them died of exposure and starvation. Historical documents show that some of the others, desperate and failing, resorted to cannibalism. Still, they pushed slowly ahead.

Suffering in the icy mountain camp, the rest of the Donner party hoped against hope that rescuers would come soon. On Christmas Day, Breen led his family in prayer, as he did every day. The situation, he wrote, was appalling, but he had trust in God. He sent his two oldest boys outside for firewood, writing that he was unable to go. In some of the other shelters, the situation was worse, but resourceful Margaret Reed had hoarded a few bits of apple, beans, and a tiny piece of bacon. She cooked the precious food for her children in honor of the day. Breen was used to cold weather from his years in Ireland, Canada, and the Territory of Iowa. But the relentless snow, by then about nine feet deep, was hard to fathom. Would it never stop? Cutting a tree was difficult because the trunk would sink deep into the drifts, making it nearly impossible to retrieve. The harsh storms, high elevation, and lack of adequate shelter and provisions were a fatal combination. The travelers began to die.

The year 1847 began cold and dark. As the gloomy January weeks stretched on, food ran out. The emigrants began cutting off pieces of the cowhide that covered their shelters and boiling them to make an unpleasant gluey substance to eat.

Breen wrote that the snow was thirteen feet deep and that their cabin was buried. In desperation, Margaret and Virginia Reed, along with two others, attempted to hike out, but were forced to return after a few days of struggling through the drifts. By then, the hides that had roofed the Reeds' shelter were gone, used for food. The Breens took the family in. Young Virginia wrote that Peggy saved her life by slipping her small bits of meat.

Meanwhile, thirty-three days after they had started out, seven members of the Forlorn Hope party, emaciated and barely alive, reached civilization near Johnson's Ranch north of Sutter's Fort. The other ten members, including the devoted Charles Stanton and cheerful Patrick Dolan, had died along the way. The survivors immediately alerted the settlers, including James Reed, to the Donner party's plight.

In mid-January, Breen wrote: *". . . provisions scarce hides are the only article we depend on. . . ."* By the first week in February, he reported that Peggy was deeply worried that their family would starve to death. There were only three hides left, a tiny amount of meat, and despairing neighbors who were gaunt and desperately hungry. Plus, they had taken in Augustus Spitzer, one of the bachelor teamsters, who was starving. Severe storms dropped even more snow, which historians believe had reached fifteen to twenty feet. The Breens' two oldest boys helped bury the dead in the drifts as, one after another, the travelers perished. Struggling from camp to camp and shelter to shelter, the remaining emigrants conferred about what to do next.

On February 8, Spitzer died. There were other miseries, too. Breen's diary mentioned that some of the group experienced frozen toes, bad headaches, a swollen jaw from a toothache, and possible food poisoning. George Donner, who had gashed his hand, was dying of infection. Fleas, bedbugs, lice, and foul odors infested the shelters. Breen himself suffered from agonizing kidney stones.

One can only imagine what the children did all winter, trapped inside the dark shelters, too weak to play. It's safe to surmise that their parents, with their last bit of energy, reassured them as best they could.

February 18 dawned clear but cold. Although Breen mentioned the day's events tersely in his diary, they were an answer to his prayers. Seven hardy rescuers struggled on foot over the snowbound summit into camp, bringing a few provisions. Their plan was to help some of the emigrants to the settlements and leave the others to wait for relief parties that were coming after them. Wasting no time, they assembled a group of twenty-three, mostly children, and set out. Two of the Breen children went along.

The remaining Breens ate the rest of their hides. Patrick Breen must have struggled with his next decision. Their dog, Towser, had accompanied them on the trip and was undoubtedly a beloved pet. Somehow the family had kept the skinny animal alive through the winter, but on February 23, Breen reported that he had shot Towser and dressed the meat. Anguished, the family swallowed the scant meals the dog provided. They continued to pray in desperation for rescue and an early spring.

March 1, 1847, was sunny, predicting the events of the day. A second relief party—led by James Reed, who had again gone to great lengths to procure animals, food, and men—labored into camp with more provisions. The time had come for the rest of the Breens to leave Truckee Lake. They would cache their few belongings and hike out with the rescuers.

Breen's diary ended on that joyous note and a final sober sentence: *". . .they say the snow will be here untill June."* Among the few items they took with them was the diary, maybe wrapped and carried inside his clothing.

The family's trials were not over. It was a long, demanding trip on foot over Donner Pass and down into the foothills and valleys. Three days out from Truckee Lake, an icy blizzard swept over the skeletal hikers. Food was nearly gone. As exhaustion overtook them, they faltered at a rugged place they later called Starved Camp. Scrambling for firewood, the group built a small campfire on a platform of green wood and huddled around it, trying to outlast the driving wind and swirling snow. Exposure, fatigue, and hunger took their toll. The Breens and several others could go no farther. They would stay and hope for a third group of rescuers. When the blizzard was finally over, the remainder of the party gathered wood for them and went on.

The deep snow beneath their fire melted, creating a cavernous abyss, and the flames sank to the bottom. Peggy Breen, at that point possibly the strongest of the

Starved Camp group, urged everyone to descend into the hole and stay close to the warmth. She doled out a tiny bit of sugar saved in her pocket to those most in need. They remained there for several days. Members of the group began to die. Historical records again show signs of cannibalism among some of the survivors as despair took over.

Breen himself was weak and sick—and most likely convinced that he and Peggy would die and lose their children to the elements. But he continued to pray. Crowded into the narrow snow shelter, he felt time crawl to a halt. Someone, perhaps Peggy, climbed from the fire pit to get more wood.

In the nick of time, a third relief party pushing toward Truckee Lake discovered the family and their companions deep in the pit, hunched over and barely alive. The rescuers quickly roused the group with food. Then they started them staggering slowly toward the settlements. One rescuer, John Stark, shuttled several of the children on his strong back, taking each a short way and going back for another, over the entire long distance. The younger Breen children reportedly were among those he carried.

Finally, after miles of slow, agonizing travel, they reached the beautiful warm valley below. To the Breens and their surviving companions, it seemed like paradise. The Breens' oldest son, John, later recalled that pleasant sunny morning at the end of their journey, with green grass surrounding him and birds singing from the branches above. He said the image was etched in his memory for life.

Revived by the established settlers with food, warmth, and sleep, the Breens reunited with their other children. The entire family had made it through; they were one of only two Donner party families who had not lost a member to death. Nearly half of their original group had perished. Eventually, all of the remaining travelers at Truckee Lake who were still alive were rescued.

Patrick and Peggy Breen and their children settled in San Juan Bautista, just south of today's city of San Jose, where they purchased a two-story adobe house near the mission. The house had been built by General José Antonio Castro, who had helped command the Mexican army during the Mexican War. Today the home still stands as a furnished museum, part of the San Juan Bautista Plaza District, a National Historic Landmark and a California State Historic Park.

Breen became a rancher, and he and Peggy lived in the spacious home with its thick walls and second-story covered porches for the rest of their lives. Another son, William, was born to them. Some historians believe they operated an inn there, welcoming travelers who needed a place to stay. The money to buy the house and surrounding land came from their son John, who went to the goldfields as a teenager and returned with a small fortune to help his family.

Breen's diary, now faded and yellow, is the only surviving first-person account written at Truckee Lake during that fateful winter. It reveals much about this complex man and the horrendous conditions he and his family endured in the Sierra Nevada as they persisted through unimaginable anguish to reach the land of their dreams. The Breens will be remembered for their perseverance and faith—and for surviving one of the most devastating pioneer journeys in history.

"A POCKET
FULL OF ROCKS"

The Story of William Swain

WILLIAM SWAIN HUGGED HIS MOTHER and begged her to take care of herself as he stood ready to depart the family's farm in western New York State. He locked eyes with his older brother, George, and shook his hand, swallowing the lump in his throat. Then he pulled his wife and baby daughter close, holding them for a long moment.

With a last look and a quiet wave, he began his 1849 journey to California.

William, twenty-seven, and George, twenty-nine, had grown up on the small farm situated near the Niagara River. Upon their father's death in 1838, the brothers and their mother, Patience, had inherited the two-story stone house and surrounding farmland. William finished his education and became a schoolteacher in Niagara County, while George developed an interest in local politics. Both of them spent long hours working in the fields.

In his mid-twenties, William married Sabrina Barrett, an educated young woman he'd met at a spelling bee. She moved into the Swains' home and, in 1848, their daughter, Eliza (or Lila), was born. Soon after that, news of California gold discoveries began to trickle in. William listened to the stories and studied the newspaper reports with George. Here, he figured, was a way to improve life for his family. But William didn't see how he could leave the farm for the gold country. Then George offered to take over all of the work while he was gone.

William prepared to go west at once.

The brothers recruited three companions to travel with him: John Root, a nineteen-year-old bachelor; Frederick Bailey, thirty, a husband and the father of a young son; and forty-three-year-old Michael Hutchinson, a farmer and widower. The four would travel by steamer from Buffalo, New York, through the Great Lakes to Chicago, and then by canal and riverboat to Independence, Missouri, their jump-off point for the overland trails. There, they would purchase a wagon and other supplies, joining the hordes of gold seekers hurrying to California.

William Swain was determined to improve his family's circumstances by making the long journey to California, where he tried his hand at mining during the Gold Rush. PHOTOGRAPH COURTESY OF BEINECKE RARE BOOK AND MANUSCRIPT LIBRARY, YALE UNIVERSITY.

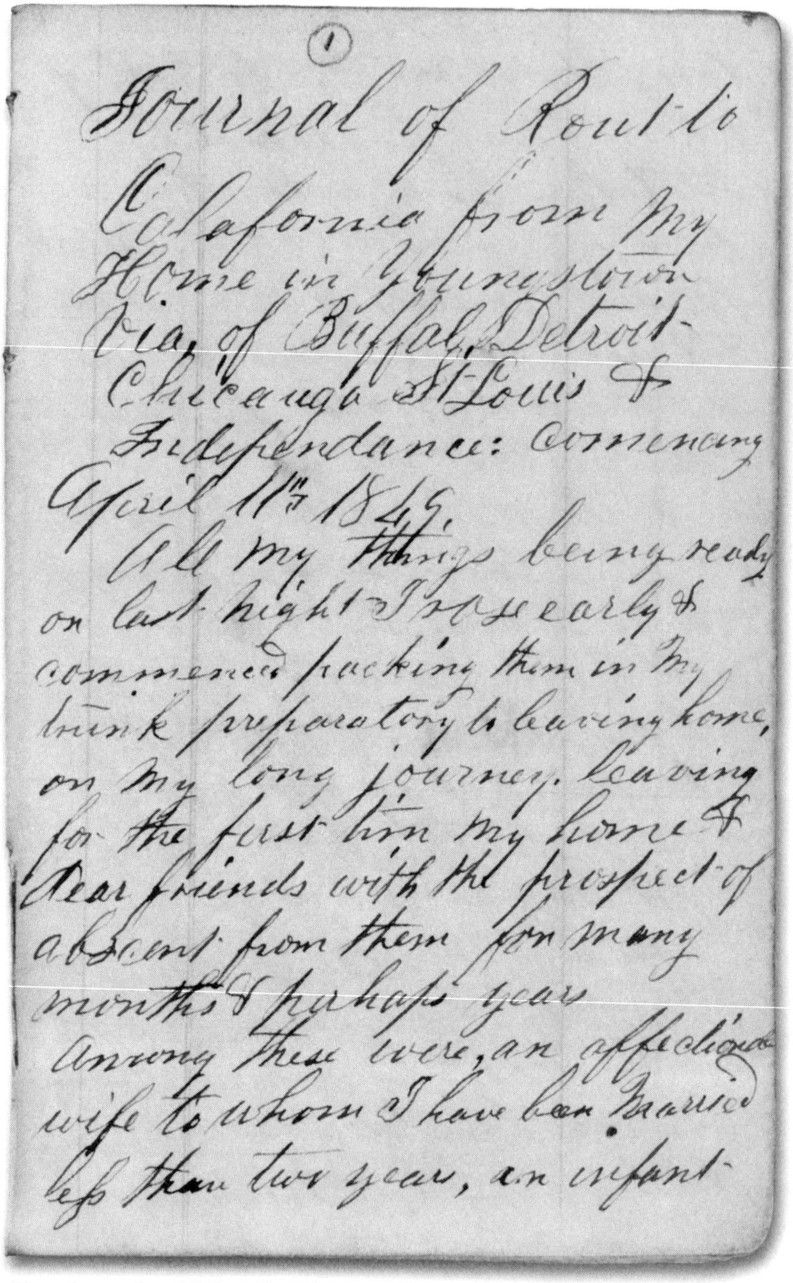

Journal of Rout to
Calafornia from My
Home in Youngstown
Via, of Buffalo, Detroit
Chicaugo St Louis &
Independance: Commencing
April 11ᵗʰ 1849.

All my things being ready
on last night I rose early &
commenced packing them in my
trunk preparatory to leaving home,
on my long journey, leaving
for the first time my home &
dear friends with the prospect of
absent from them for many
months & perhaps years

Among these were, an affectiond
wife to whom I have been Married
less than two years, an infant

This title page from William Swain's journal illustrates how pioneers often wrote in small script from margin to margin to save paper. PHOTOGRAPH COURTESY OF BEINECKE RARE BOOK AND MANUSCRIPT LIBRARY, YALE UNIVERSITY.

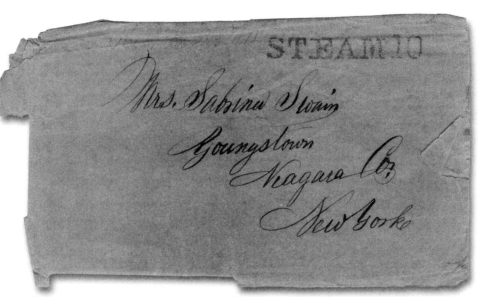

William Swain wrote long letters to his wife and family during his 1849 trip to the California goldfields, although some never reached their destination. PHOTOGRAPH COURTESY OF BEINECKE RARE BOOK AND MANUSCRIPT LIBRARY, YALE UNIVERSITY.

When he got to Buffalo, Swain began sending letters home. He also kept a diary, recording each day's travel in a small, leather-bound volume. While he often described his yearning to be back with his loved ones, he also wrote of his commitment to the trip west. His goal was to return with enough gold to ease his family's circumstances.

The four travel partners endured three long weeks of boat travel before nearing Independence. During that time, they got to know a disciplined company of men from Michigan called the Wolverine Rangers, who were also heading to the goldfields. After reaching their jump-off destination, the four joined the Rangers' ranks for a fee of one hundred dollars each and a newly purchased wagon. The joint-stock company consisted of eighteen covered wagons and more than sixty men led by an elected board of directors and a team of officers.

The Rangers set out on the Santa Fe Trail on May 16, 1849. It was a late start for a California-bound wagon train, but they weren't concerned. At first, they traveled easily over the plains, but rain and overuse by heavily loaded wagons soon turned the trail to mud. The men turned west to join the California Trail, fanning out to dodge the worst ruts.

Cholera outbreaks plagued the emigrants on the crowded trails, where graves dotted the roadsides. With no knowledge of the disease's bacterial cause, which had not yet been discovered, the travelers tried to outrun the horrifying illness, little realizing that they carried it with them. Those infected often perished within hours of being afflicted with its agonizing symptoms: vomiting, diarrhea, muscle cramps, and terrible thirst. Swain was highly aware of cholera. He continually reassured his family that he was evading it, but mentioned that others had died from the disease.

As spring rains drenched Swain and his fellow travelers, he reported that high winds on the prairie were common. Despite the weather, he appreciated the beauty of the sweeping plains, green grasslands, and vast skies surrounding him. He took long moments to enjoy the views from hilltops and the edges of tablelands—and tried to describe the landscape to the folks back home. Writing by candlelight, he told them he was using the *"tops of our trunks"* for an uncomfortable desk. Another time he wrote to Sabrina on paper so wet he almost couldn't use it. In his diary, he jotted close to the narrow margins in small, evenly slanted handwriting to preserve space.

Swain's family, hearing about the cholera on the trails, went to the post office every day, anxiously awaiting word from him. If his letters were delayed, they agonized. When a note finally arrived, they hung on every word, trying to decipher his mood by reading between the lines, and they shared the news with his companions' friends and families. They wrote back faithfully, begging him to come home if he took ill, assuring him they'd rather have him healthy than gain the wealth he sought for them. Sabrina confided that her anxieties for him were *"beyond description."* Their letters were sent to the few established outposts along the trail.

The company took advantage of a ferry crossing on the Kansas River where they found good feed for the animals and abundant wood for campfires. Even with a boat, it took great physical labor to get the wagons and animals across the swollen waters. Afterward, Swain wrote of being tired and sore.

Then came the day he'd feared. On May 31, he was attacked by severe dysentery. Swain almost certainly wondered if he'd contracted cholera, and if he, too, would succumb to the excruciating death he had seen in others. His companions were sympathetic, and the company doctor was helpful. Swain took remedies that ranged from opium to a *"dose of rhubarb"* to a mustard plaster, but nothing helped for long. He reported getting sicker and weaker until he had to ride in the jolting wagon or on horseback as the company pressed on toward Fort Kearny, which had been established a year earlier. Nearly two weeks later, he was still taking the prescribed medicines.

But Swain was destined to finish his journey to California. He slowly recovered. He regretted lost opportunities to send letters home, but was grateful that he felt good enough to bathe and mend and wash his clothes. Throughout his illness, he kept up his journal entries, and when the wagon train reached the fort, he resumed his letters. He sent them by any means possible, including traders and returning travelers.

The trail between Fort Kearny on the Platte River and Fort Laramie on the North Platte, a distance of more than three hundred miles, was relatively good, so the emigrants could cover twenty or more miles a day. By then, many wagon companies had seen incompetent leadership or conflict among members. Segments had split off in discord to travel separately. The Wolverine Rangers faced little of this. In general, they stayed true to the *Articles of Association and Agreement* they had drawn up before embarking on the trail. Their members got along unusually well, and the leadership was effective. Often, they stopped for the Sabbath. Not wasting time on petty quarrels, the company advanced at a good pace. They were at the end of the year's migration, though, and found the trail strewn with castoff belongings from earlier wagon trains. The grass was shorn and trampled; the water fouled.

Bison and antelope were plentiful. Swain stood on his wagon tongue and drove with one hand to catch sight of his first buffalo. A hastily organized hunt was unsuccessful, but the next day the men tried again. They ended up with meat for supper and abundant reserves of jerky hanging from the wagons.

The Rangers experienced a violent hailstorm that Swain described in detail, from alarming bolts of lightning to egg-sized hailstones. The men outlasted it by managing the stampeding animals and taking cover in the wagons. Some wore cooking pots on their heads to protect themselves. After the storm subsided, they had welts, bruises, and black eyes. The cattle suffered, too, with cuts on their backs and hips. Some of the wagons were damaged. Undaunted, the Rangers set things right as best they could. Then they gathered hailstones for a rare treat: ice water.

Swain reported that they were eight miles from Fort Laramie on the Fourth of July. The company stopped to celebrate with patriotic music, prayers, a reading

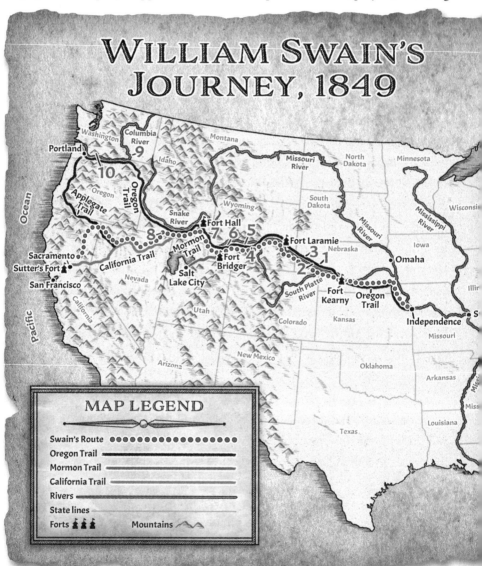

WILLIAM SWAIN'S JOURNEY, 1849

MAP LEGEND

Swain's Route	●●●●●●●●●●●●●●●●
Oregon Trail	
Mormon Trail	
California Trail	
Rivers	
State lines	
Forts ▲▲▲	Mountains ⌃

of the Declaration of Independence, and a stirring speech. An elaborate ham dinner was served, and later there were rousing toasts with brandy. Swain stayed for a few toasts but, unhappy with the others' rowdy behavior, retired to his tent to write a letter to Sabrina. He mailed it the next day at the fort. In the letter, he told her that he was doing well, but that he would *"advise no man to come this way to California."*

LANDMARK LEGEND

1. Courthouse Rock
2. Chimney Rock
3. Scotts Bluff
4. Independence Rock
5. Devil's Gate
6. South Pass
7. Soda Springs
8. City of Rocks
9. The Whitman Mission
10. The Dalles

The trail got harder. West of Fort Laramie, the landscape turned steep, with rocky ground that slashed the animals' hooves. After difficulty crossing the North Platte, the travelers encountered a long stretch of desert-like terrain with sagebrush and pools of toxic alkali water. The company kept on, enduring choking dust, poor grass, and deep sand that made pulling the wagons exhausting.

The trail led to the Sweetwater River, a welcome relief for its fresh, life-giving water, and then rose gradually to the famous South Pass. Cholera all but vanished, much to the emigrants' relief. Less congestion on the trail, the high altitude and arid climate, and access to clean running water like the Sweetwater probably played a part. At the same time, opportunities to send letters home diminished. This far into the journey, the remote outposts that offered mail service dwindled.

Soon after passing Devil's Gate, Swain reported getting sick again with fever and diarrhea. He described his fellow travelers as so *"blunted by weariness"* that they couldn't help much. Again, he had to ride in the wagon and missed writing diary entries for a few days. After suffering for more than a week, he regained his strength.

The Rangers took Sublette's Cutoff in today's southwest Wyoming. Sometimes traveling at night to avoid the searing sun, the company crossed fifty miles of dry, desolate country to the Green River, arriving on August 4. Swain told of helping give medicine to an ill companion, but the man was too sick to recover. His death sobered the company, and Swain was struck by a fresh bout of homesickness and a renewed appreciation for all he had left behind.

The group continued into the beautiful Bear River Valley, which was rich with grass, water, and stunning mountain views. Then they veered onto the new Hudspeth's Cutoff in present-day Idaho. But reports about the shortcut were contradictory, and the travelers realized they didn't know exactly where they were. With no other choice, they followed the faint tracks into the distance.

One of Swain's original three companions from New York, John Root, grew discouraged with the Rangers' slow progress and decided to strike out on his own. The company bought him out, and Root left the group on August 26 with a pony or two and a few pounds of provisions. Swain sent along a letter for Sabrina, asking Root to mail it when he reached the settlements.

The company merged with the main California Trail near the City of Rocks, an unusual cluster of stone formations in today's southern Idaho that looked to the homesick emigrants like urban buildings. Relieved to know where they were, they inched toward the Humboldt River. Nine more members of the wagon train broke away to travel more quickly. The remaining men, trudging for three weeks in the dust and dung along the riverbank, suffered with the animals. Grass was scarce, but the river provided water of sorts. The Rangers made progress by again traveling at night to avoid the daytime heat. Swain was temporarily sick with chest pains, a pounding head, and a backache, but he continued to write in his journal, even though each tedious day was the same.

By the time they reached the Applegate Trail turnoff in today's northwestern Nevada, which led to the new Lassen Trail, the weather had cooled. Daytime travel was possible again, and the nights were cold. Swain told of bathing in the river to remove the itchy alkali dust from his skin. The men cut hay to store in the wagons for the stretch of trail ahead—the most barren and desolate yet. Beyond the desert lay the rugged Sierra Nevada, where late crossings were dangerous.

By then it was mid-September.

The Applegate-Lassen route seemed the best choice, but in reality, it was a desperately long and difficult trail. The exhausted Rangers tackled the arid wilderness by inching their way between widely spaced, meager springs and once more traveling at night. Swain continued his diary, despite the slow, arduous travel. Thoughts of Sabrina, his baby daughter, his mother, and George kept him going. He was sure that the trail was headed relentlessly northwest, away from California. October approached. It was too late to turn back and take a more established route.

The company persevered. The ghastly bodies of dead cattle fouled some of the infrequent springs. As their own animals failed, the Rangers got separated. They threw out their prized but heavy blacksmith equipment and sent reinforcements back to the stragglers. Reunited, they moved toward the mountains with only about a dozen wagons. As they got closer, the weather turned colder and the desert gradually became foothills. Game reappeared. Swain reported grass and water and icy nights. The summit of the Sierra Nevada was within reach.

Or was it?

Historical records show that the high mountains the Rangers crossed in mid-October were the Warner Range near Goose Lake in today's northeast corner of California, not the Sierra Nevada. Swain had been correct in his conviction that the trail had been leading them north. The Lassen Trail then abruptly veered south toward the goldfields, but the settlements on the other side of the Sierras were still more than two hundred miles away.

The United States Army agents in California knew the peril of being stranded in the mountains for the winter. The Donner party's horrendous ordeal three years earlier had proved that late crossings could be fatal. Now, hearing about stragglers along the overland trails, the agents organized relief parties. With help from others, they methodically set out to distribute supplies to the depleted travelers, including the Rangers. They also informed them about the correct distance ahead and urged them to abandon their possessions and hurry to the settlements.

The Rangers immediately voted to divide up the company property and disband. The men amicably split into small groups with one or two wagons apiece to cross the mountains before heavy snow blocked the way. Swain, his two remaining partners from home, and a farmer from Michigan started out together with one wagon and a few skeletal oxen. Worn to the bone, they followed the Pit River into the wild jumble of mountains ahead.

The last two weeks of October were among the worst of the journey. Rocks and huge boulders made parts of the road nearly impassable. The Lassen Trail required intense physical effort from the tired men and animals. Fortunately, Swain's group rejoined some of the other Rangers and encountered a second relief party distributing provisions.

Swain's diary abruptly ended on October 30. From other travelers' accounts and Swain's later recollections, it is known that the group toiled over the rough terrain as drenching rain turned to snow. Finally, they ditched all but two of their wagons, leaving their belongings behind in their pitched tents. Wet, numb, and discouraged, some stayed with the wagons and oxen. The others, like Swain, went ahead on foot carrying on their backs what little they'd kept. In a dangerous snowstorm, they followed a long ridgetop that would lead down to the Sacramento River Valley. By then, they were fleeing for their lives. It was November 6.

They descended into pouring rain. Finally, on November 8, ragged, dirty, wet, and emaciated, they arrived at their destination: Lassen's Ranch near today's Vina, California.

A few days later, Swain and Frederick Bailey, one of his original partners, started on foot for the Feather River diggings, a distance of about fifty miles. There they planned to meet their third partner, Michael Hutchinson, who had ridden his horse from the mountain summit to scout mining possibilities there.

Back home, no one had heard from Swain since he was at Fort Laramie on the Fourth of July, four months earlier. Worry for his safety consumed them, but they kept up their letter-writing. Sabrina told of her anguish in thinking harm may have come to him and her struggle to keep her spirits up. George reiterated their anxiety, telling his brother that no one would think less of him if he simply came home. Today, historians know that the family received no news of him until mid-April, 1850. The letter Swain sent with his friend John Root never reached them, although Root himself made it safely to the goldfields. Neither did Swain's letter telling of his safe arrival in California.

Swain, Bailey, and Hutchinson, along with two others, set up a mining partnership, filed a claim, and built a sturdy log cabin on the bank of the South Fork of the Feather River. There, they waited out the rainy season, while the river frothed and raged. Diverting the stream and mining its bed, where gold was usually found, was impossible until spring. Stuck in the windowless hut for the winter, the group fared better than most of the miners, many of whom weathered the long months in leaky canvas tents or primitive brush shelters.

In his letters home, Swain reported astronomical prices for food and supplies, and reassured his family that he had not lost sight of his principles amid the depravity in the swarming mining camps. He read his Bible, wrote letters, and when the weather permitted, roamed the hills panning the streambanks for gold. Occasionally he was rewarded with a small find.

This sturdy log cabin is similar to the one William Swain described in his journal as his gold camp dwelling. COURTESY OF THE CALIFORNIA HISTORY ROOM, CALIFORNIA STATE LIBRARY, SACRAMENTO, CALIFORNIA.

Swain assured his brother that life in California was *"a dog's life."* He urged George to tell those planning an overland journey to stay home. His writings also described the plight of California's native peoples, whose country was now inundated with thousands of miners claiming the land for their own. Brutal acts against them, Swain said, were enough to *"make humanity weep. . . ."*

Much to his discouragement, Swain did not receive word from home. The postal service to California was agonizingly slow. Although mail did arrive in the larger cities after traveling through Panama, it poured in with such volume that letters often couldn't be found when a miner made the lengthy trip to retrieve them. Finally, in March of 1850, Swain ecstatically reported that he'd received letters from home, ten months after leaving. He was profoundly relieved to read that his family was safe and well.

For the next year, Swain tried and failed to find the gold that would enhance his family's future. When the claim on the South Fork failed to produce much, he tried other locations. The backbreaking labor kept him strong, but conditions in the camps were squalid. He again wrote of being sick and feverish. During the summer, when the best mining could be done, hot weather made digging miserable. Most of the lucrative areas had already been panned out. As the weeks stretched on, Swain realized that he, like thousands of others, was not going to reach his goal. He had assured Sabrina that he would return with *"a pocket full of rocks,"* but now it seemed unlikely. In October 1850, after nearly a year of laborious effort, he decided to go home, bringing his small profit of $700 or $800.

Almost no one took the overland trails east. Instead, they went by ship to Nicaragua or Panama, struggled across the Isthmus, and traveled again by sea to the States. Swain was worried about cholera aboard the sailing ship he selected in San Francisco and violence on the route through Panama, so he wrote his final wishes to George in case he didn't survive the voyage.

The trip began well, with safe but slow passage on a sailing ship to Panama, where he arrived on Christmas Day. Swain traversed the Isthmus, writing about the tropical scenery and foods, but shortly before boarding the *Falcon* for New York, he fell ill with a type of malaria called Chagres fever. Desperately sick during the long sea journey, he arrived in New York in late January so feeble he had to be helped from the ship.

He telegraphed George, who traveled to his side right away. Swain began recovering, and the two journeyed home for his joyous reunion with Sabrina, their little daughter, and Patience on February 6, 1851. Neighbors and friends gathered to welcome the forty-niner back. Later, all three of Swain's original travel companions also returned safely.

William Swain enjoyed a long life on the family farm. He and George bought more acreage and planted peaches, which thrived. Sabrina, overjoyed to have her husband home, worked beside them. In the years that followed, two sons and another daughter were born.

Grateful that his life had been spared on his twenty-two-month sojourn to California, Swain and his family cherished the letters they'd exchanged during those treacherous days. Along with his detailed diary, the letters served as a poignant reminder of his perilous trip west—and the unbreakable bonds that called him home.

SKETCHING
THE WAY WEST

The Story of James F. Wilkins

JAMES F. WILKINS KNEW that traveling the California Trail in 1849 wouldn't be easy. People were hurrying west on the dangerous overland road in hordes, hoping to strike it rich in the newly discovered California goldfields. Wilkins didn't have gold fever like the others. He wanted to be the first to sketch scenes from the epic journey, return home, and paint a massive, scrolling panorama from his drafts. Other artists were making small fortunes traveling the country with similar murals, narrating them to the enthusiastic public. If he could be the first to present a grand spooling vista of the overland trail, certainly people would flock to his show, where he would share the beauty of the western landscapes. He kept his plan to himself, careful not to give others the same idea.

Wilkins was born in 1808 in England, where he began his art career. Little is known about his early life other than his connection to London's famed Royal Academy, where he exhibited his work. He moved to the United States in the 1830s, settling first in Peoria, Illinois, and then in St. Louis. There he became known for his lifelike portraits.

In the spring of 1849, he said goodbye to his wife and daughters and took a riverboat from St. Louis to an overland trail jump-off spot at Weston, Missouri. After a false start there, he and a few others traveled up the Missouri River to a location opposite Old Fort Kearny. Wilkins had collected the necessities for the trip, including a leather-bound pocket diary and one or two sketchbooks, along with paintbrushes and other art supplies. His plan was to make watercolor field sketches of the sights he witnessed along the way, and keep a detailed journal.

He joined a party using oxen to pull their covered wagons, possibly reasoning that their slower pace would allow him time to work on his drawings. The group began its long trek in mid-May. That meant that crowds of wagon travelers had started out ahead of them, their animals shearing the grass for miles surrounding the trail.

Wilkins seemed to adapt quickly to the rigors of the trail. He walked the long daily distances, hoping to buy a horse later in the journey from the native peoples they encountered. The artist tolerated being drenched, exhausted, and hungry, only mildly mentioning them in his diary. He wrote long paragraphs every two or three days—cryptic penciled entries in which he used first initials to identify fellow travelers. Throughout the journal there are hints that he may have been a private man who was peaceful, determined, and purposeful. A portrait he painted of himself depicts strong, handsome facial features and thinning dark hair.

By the end of May, Wilkins was already foot-sore, but was getting used to the demands of an overland trip. Somehow, he managed to keep up with the many tasks of wagon travel, write in his journal, and paint monochrome sketches. A small mark in his diary indicated each location where he created a drawing.

The weather was cold and wet. The buffalo chips used for making fires were soaked and useless. During an especially intense thunderstorm, Wilkins drew

James F. Wilkins painted this oil-on-canvas self-portrait, but is best known for the sketches he made of his 1849 overland journey during the California Gold Rush. PHOTOGRAPH COURTESY OF MISSOURI HISTORICAL SOCIETY COLLECTIONS.

night duty, guarding the group and its sixteen wagons as strong winds blew torrents of rain across the unprotected plains of present-day Nebraska. He was undoubtedly chilled and drenched to the skin. It was an experience he called *"one of the disagreeables of the trip."*

Standing guard was one of the wagon train's most essential duties, but also among the least popular. Robbing much-needed rest from the unlucky men

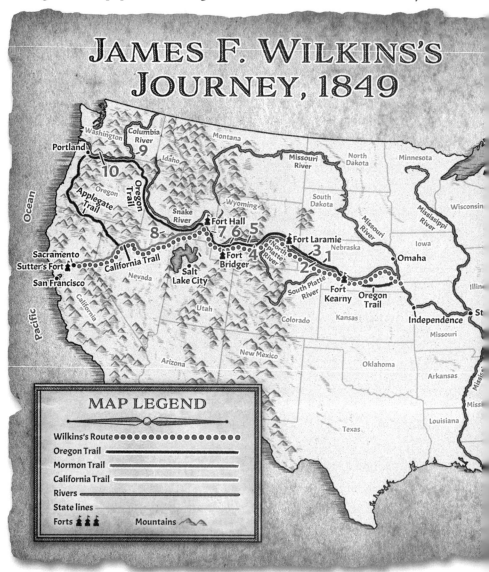

JAMES F. WILKINS'S JOURNEY, 1849

MAP LEGEND

Wilkins's Route ●●●●●●●●●●●●●●●
Oregon Trail
Mormon Trail
California Trail
Rivers
State lines
Forts 🛉🛉🛉   Mountains ⌂⌂

whose turn it was to watch over the camp, night duty carried the responsibility of protecting the stock from predators and preventing stampedes. A careless guard could cost the emigrants days of lost travel as they searched for scattered animals.

Cholera wracked other travelers, but Wilkins and his companions initially stayed well. The farther they went, the more graves they encountered. Finally, the feared illness reached their party. In mid-June, one man fell gravely ill. Wilkins noted that cholera was *"becoming very alarming, and causes serious uneasiness in the camp."* Their companion barely survived.

By the end of June, the group had traveled up the Platte River as far as Fort Laramie. Wilkins noted that others were abandoning their cumbersome wagons and loading their belongings onto mules in an attempt to reach California faster. Rumors about bad roads and lack of grass ahead were disturbing, but Wilkins and his wagon party pressed on. As they neared the Laramie Mountains, known in 1849 as the Black Hills, he described their shadowy detail in his journal. Gazing on the red cliffs and desolate black rocks interspersed with gray-green sagebrush, he stopped again to sketch.

Although the trail was hilly and steep in places, the group made good progress. His companions, covered with layers of dust, grumbled about the dearth of grass. With a raft made of five bound-together dugout canoes offered for a fee by a local settler, the men ferried the wagons to the opposite side of the Platte, hoping to find better feed. But the struggle to provide for the animals continued.

LANDMARK LEGEND

1. Courthouse Rock	6. South Pass
2. Chimney Rock	7. Soda Springs
3. Scotts Bluff	8. City of Rocks
4. Independence Rock	9. The Whitman Mission
5. Devil's Gate	10. The Dalles

Wilkins sketched this view of the Black Hills (known today as the Laramie Mountains) as his wagon party traversed the difficult terrain. PHOTOGRAPH COURTESY OF WISCONSIN HISTORICAL SOCIETY, WHI-31284.

The Fourth of July was a day like any other for Wilkins. His holiday dinner was a *"piece of hard sea bread and a tin cup of indifferent water."* The bleak countryside didn't lend itself to stopping, so the company pushed on to the Sweetwater River in present-day central Wyoming, dodging poisonous alkali springs and enduring grit that blew into their faces. Despite his earlier plans, Wilkins had been unable to purchase a horse to ride.

The artist appreciated the unique Sweetwater country and made a point to sketch Independence Rock and Devil's Gate, among other scenes. He wrote that he wanted to stay longer at Devil's Gate to add detail to his drawing, but the party needed to move on. Nevertheless, his rough portrayal accurately captured the vertical rocky gap in the cliffs and the river running through it. When the group caught sight of the magnificent snowcapped peaks of the Wind River Range, Wilkins was again ready with his paints.

Wilkins wanted to add more detail to his sketch of Devil's Gate and the Sweetwater River, but his companions were intent upon moving on. PHOTOGRAPH COURTESY OF WISCONSIN HISTORICAL SOCIETY, WHI-31291.

He never mentioned where he kept his sketchbooks, but it's likely they were wrapped in canvas or similar cloth and stowed where they had the least chance of getting damaged. He might have stored them in the wagons—or perhaps he carried them on his person. Water stains, either from treacherous river crossings or a drenching rain, would ruin his drawings. Dust could discolor the pages or render the pictures less distinct. Keeping paper materials safe was a challenge for all. Some emigrants wedged their Bibles in the overhead wagon bows while crossing streams; others had trunks to keep treasured belongings dry.

On July 14, Wilkins reported being sick with a headache, loss of appetite, and chills—an illness suspected to have been the tick-borne disease they called mountain fever. He struggled for days with weakness and fatigue, but was able to keep up with the company by riding a shared horse. They crossed the Great Divide at South Pass.

Trouble struck when the group's horses got lost. Animals often wandered off, bolted from fright, or were stolen from emigrant trains. This time, the horses couldn't be found, and the company decided to move on without them. Wilkins, drained of energy, had to keep up on foot. Somehow, he walked from the Big Sandy River to the Green River, a distance of about forty miles. His party forded the Green on a perilous, leaky ferry.

It wasn't until July 23, ten days after he fell ill, that he reported feeling better. Much to his relief, he was able to purchase a mule from a man he met as the party approached Fort Bridger. The animal made it possible for him to ride again, and he could explore the countryside for the best scenes to draw.

Even in late July, nights were frosty at Fort Bridger. Prices were inflated. Despite the rich grass and clear, cold water, the group didn't linger. Soon after

Fort Bridger, shown in this Wilkins sketch, had been built in 1842-43 and served as a resupply station for early pioneers. PHOTOGRAPH COURTESY OF WISCONSIN HISTORICAL SOCIETY, WHI-31549.

leaving the fort, Wilkins had dismounted to sketch a scene, and his new mule got away. While the artist was capturing him again, the animal kicked him hard in the jaw. Bleeding and in pain, Wilkins worried that his jaw was broken, but the injury turned out to be minor.

The company traveled on to the Bear River Valley, grateful to have excellent feed and water for the animals. Wilkins took artistic note of the reddish bluffs along the river. Farther down the trail, the effervescent springs in today's southeastern Idaho captured his imagination. He made half a dozen watercolor sketches and wrote detailed descriptions of the unusual features. The travelers drank the bubby water, a novelty and a rare treat.

In early August, they took the Hudspeth Cutoff to shave off miles, but were initially disappointed by the rough condition of the trail. It was hard to find information about good camping places; the trail was so new that none of the overland guidebooks included it yet. Along the cutoff, Wilkins traded with a small party of native Snake people for moccasins and trousers, using some of his paints as barter.

The group had no choice but to press on. Battling uncertainty, thirst, suffocating dust, and cacti underfoot, they emerged onto the Old Fort Hall road, disappointed to find that the shortcut had saved them only a few miles. Wilkins's disappointment was short-lived, though, because they entered the City of Rocks, where he was intrigued by the unusual clusters of giant boulders. Sketching in his usual monochrome gray, he recorded their curious shapes.

Merging with the main route (the *great thorofare,* as Wilkins put it), the emigrants soon drew near the northeast corner of present-day Nevada, where the trail stretched to the Humboldt River. Again, the vegetation had been shorn to the ground. Wilkins's party had to drive their oxen for a mile or more out of the way to find feed. Travel was unpleasant, with powdery dust that settled on everything, desolate stretches without water, and a monotonous diet of bacon day after day. Tempers were short and moods were sullen. The artist reported again that he stood night guard, which he disliked above all else. His spirits rebounded on August 20 near the Thousand Springs Valley when the party reached the confluence of two streams—one hot and one cold. The waters combined to create the perfect temperature for bathing. Wilkins relished the warm bath he took there, finally relaxing and washing away the grit.

On August 21, the group reached a deep spring which formed the headwaters of the Humboldt. The crystal-clear water held promise, but the most tedious section of the trail lay ahead. Wilkins lamented the irritability among his fellow travelers. Even his mule seemed out of sorts, taking off at a run with the artist on his back and nearly throwing him off.

In spite of it all, Wilkins continued to sketch the passing landscape. News of another cutoff encouraged the group in late August, as the wearisome trail down the Humboldt stretched on. Hearing that the new route shortened the distance to the northern California diggings—but lengthened the distance to the larger settlements—Wilkins supported taking the established trail, as did the majority of his party. This would take them along the well-trod route to the Humboldt Sink, across the Forty Mile Desert, and over the Sierra Nevada at today's Carson Canyon. They moved on, always searching for grass.

At the beginning of September, Wilkins opened his last can of lobster—something he probably brought all the way from St. Louis—and savored the contents. He mentioned in his diary that scurvy was becoming widespread. His company's dried fruit and vinegar were gone; all that was left of their provisions was hard bread and old bacon.

Wilkins made several sketches near the Humboldt Sink as the great desert loomed ahead. After cutting a supply of hay and filling every container with water, the party started across, traveling at night to avoid the daytime heat. It was forty miles to the Carson River, the next source of water. Covering long stretches, they worked their way across the arid, desolate terrain, distressed by the many abandoned wagons and dead cattle they saw. Finally, in an area of deep sand, their own oxen failed. Wilkins and a companion left the group and rode on, eventually reaching the river. Tired out, hungry, and thirsty, they ate a small snack they'd brought along and camped beside another company's blazing campfire.

Over the next couple of days, the group's stalled cattle were driven to the river, leaving the wagons behind in the desert. Wilkins helped as best he could, but scurvy had begun to attack him: He had the classic symptoms of fatigue, bleeding gums, and skin discoloration. Still, he continued sketching. The party let the oxen rest and rehydrate before they went back to fetch the wagons. Then they cut more hay and set out again. It is possible the artist sold his mule at the river and continued with his companions on foot.

After a few days, they reached the mouth of Carson Canyon, which led to the high pass over the Sierra Nevada. The route was known for huge boulders and slabs of rock that blocked the trail; getting wagons through was nearly impossible. The steep, rugged canyon was six miles long, a tangle of boulders and brush. As they wrestled the terrain, Wilkins made quick, rough drawings between bouts of putting his shoulder to the wheel.

Two mountain summits awaited. The next day, September 26, the party stalled. On the precipitous trail, they had to unload and carry their belongings to the top before they could get the wagons through. Reaching the final crest, Wilkins paused to appreciate the view and sketch, but an icy storm sent the party hurrying down the other side to camp.

Less than a week from his destination, Wilkins related an event that nearly killed him. A loaded gun in the wagon ahead jostled from its place and exploded, firing its ball between him and his nearest companion. Wilkins wrote only a few sentences about the near-disaster, but noted that brutal injuries and deaths had occurred along the trail from such accidents.

Fighting a rough road, wandering cattle, and exhaustion, the company struggled through the last miles to the California settlements. Finally, on October 4, after 151 days of travel, they arrived at the diggings near the mining camp later known as Placerville.

Wilkins wanted to try his hand at working the gold deposits, but stayed firm in his plan to hurry home and begin his panorama. He made sketches of the area and then traveled to Sacramento, arriving on October 16. Historians speculate that he may have earned money for the journey home by painting a mural in a prominent saloon there before moving on to San Francisco. On December 1, he began his return trip to St. Louis by ship, traveling through Panama and arriving home in late January or early February 1850. He carried with him approximately two hundred unsigned watercolor sketches.

Tragedy and hardship greeted him. His wife had died of cholera in his absence, and his property had been sold to *"pay the debts of others,"* as he put it. Wilkins grieved over this distressing news, but was able to adhere to his long-held purpose. He began working on his gigantic mural, which he called a "moving mirror" before anyone else could create a similar painting.

Enormous panoramas were popular in the 1840s and 50s. Painted on lightweight canvas-like fabric, they were hundreds of feet long and often from eight to twelve feet high, usually depicting scenes from battles or compelling current events. Eager audiences of paying customers viewed these murals, which scrolled by on a stage or in a large building and were frequently narrated by the artist. A pianist sometimes accompanied the presentation as the reels unfurled. Typically, these grand panoramas traveled from city to city, gaining fame and earning money for their creators.

It is almost certain that Wilkins had help painting his mural. Such an immense project could not be completed quickly by just one artist. With the single-minded determination he had shown on the overland trail, Wilkins pushed the project to completion. By mid-September 1850, about six months after it was begun, the masterpiece was finished.

Crowds in Peoria and St. Louis turned out to see his work. Reviews were glowing, praising Wilkins's artistic talent and accuracy. One report noted that people returned again and again to view the series of three moving scrolls. Another hinted that the scenes were so beautifully rendered and true to life that viewers felt as if they were traveling the overland trail themselves.

It was expensive to show the panorama and move the scrolls from city to city, as Wilkins tried to do. Historians believe his profit was likely moderate. Although little is known about the exact path of the moving mirror, it showed up in a few nearby cities before disappearing from the record. By 1854, Wilkins had returned to his steady art of portraiture, and at some point, he remarried.

James F. Wilkins continued to pursue art for the rest of his life. Much of his work has been lost to history, but fifty of his overland sketches and his trail diary resurfaced after many years. Wilkins probably assumed that his journal and modest watercolor drawings would be of no interest to anyone but himself.

Instead, they have become a rare, highly valued record of the 1849 trail to California. His sometimes-hasty sketches, often done under duress, became the remarkable legacy of a talented man who had the courage and persistence to carry out his ambitious dreams.

UNDAUNTED

The Story of Alvin Aaron Coffey

THE TOWN OF ST. JOSEPH, Missouri, bustled with commotion as Alvin Aaron Coffey muscled heavy canvas bags of flour into the wagon. Emigrants from all over the country were getting ready to cross the Missouri River and set off on the long, difficult journey to California. It was May 1849, and the rush to the goldfields was on. St. Joseph's muddy streets were crowded with hurried travelers, barking dogs, oxen, wagons laden with supplies, and merchants selling their wares.

Alvin Coffey, who was in his mid-twenties, had been born into slavery in Kentucky. Historical accounts differ, but it is clear that a few years before, he had been acquired by Dr. William Bassett, a physician who was leading a train of about twenty wagons west. Sources say the two had entered into an agreement: Coffey would drive Bassett's wagon over the long, treacherous distance, but once in California, he would be permitted to mine enough gold to purchase his freedom.

Driving ox teams was exhausting work. Some emigrants drove from the wagon seat, but most walked the daily miles alongside their animals, enduring whatever harsh conditions the trail produced. When they finally reached camp each night, the animals had to be unhitched, watered, and led to the best grass. Before dawn the next day, they needed to be rounded up and hitched again.

Coffey left his wife, Mahala Tindall Coffey, and their young children, Mary, John, and Lavinia, behind in Missouri. (Another son, William, had died as a toddler.) As Coffey drove the lumbering oxen over the green prairies that spring, his thoughts were undoubtedly with his family and his dreams of freedom for them all.

Almost immediately after leaving St. Joseph, one of the travelers sickened and died of cholera. Hoping to escape its lethal grip, which killed hundreds of people along the Missouri River that year, the wagon drivers urged their plodding teams to quicken their pace along the trail not understanding that the disease traveled with them.

Despite the pastoral beauty of the springtime prairies, the trip was fraught with hardship. Later in his life, Alvin Coffey recorded his reminiscences of the expedition (a rare, first-person account by a Black American pioneer). At least one other emigrant in the same wagon train, Israel F. Hale, wrote a detailed diary. The two narratives offer a glimpse into the travelers' daily struggles.

Alvin Aaron Coffey, shown in this undated photograph, succeeded in gaining freedom for himself and his family after emigrating to California. Later he became the first African American member of the California Society of Pioneers. PORTRAIT OF ALVIN COFFEY, AFRICAN AMERICAN MUSEUM & LIBRARY AT OAKLAND PHOTOGRAPH COLLECTION, MS189, AFRICAN AMERICAN MUSEUM AND LIBRARY AT OAKLAND, OAKLAND PUBLIC LIBRARY. OAKLAND, CALIFORNIA.

Coffey's work on the trail encompassed more than just the difficult task of driving. He almost certainly took care of William Bassett, who was sick for much of the journey with a serious, unknown illness. Clearing roads, hunting game for food, caring for the livestock, and repairing the wagon were all tasks that likely would have fallen to him. He also stood guard at night, taking turns with the other men. It is possible that Coffey drew guard duty with Israel Hale's teenage son, Titus, since the two developed a lifelong friendship.

When the emigrants' boots and shoes needed repair, Coffey fixed them, having learned cobbling skills earlier in his life. Many an overland pioneer needed shoe and boot repair, since the arid climate of the West shrank and loosened the wooden pegs used to hold them together.

Muddy roads, frigid temperatures, and no wood for campfires made the group's early days on the trail miserable. High wind hurled icy rain into the wagons

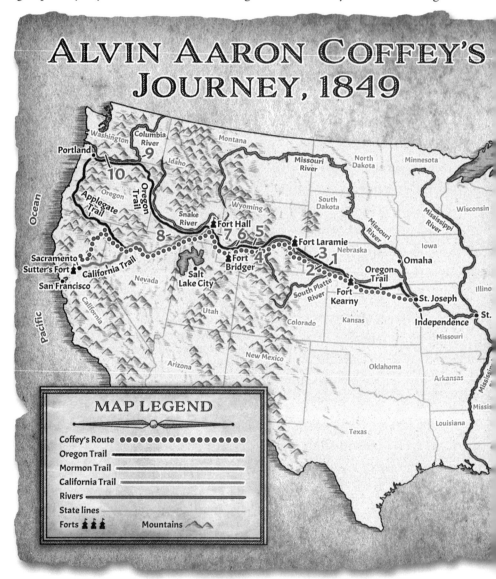

ALVIN AARON COFFEY'S JOURNEY, 1849

MAP LEGEND

Coffey's Route	●●●●●●●●●●●●●●●
Oregon Trail	
Mormon Trail	
California Trail	
Rivers	
State lines	
Forts	Mountains

and soaked their belongings. Diarist Hale reported: *"The cold weather for some days past has given a great number of our emigrants bad colds, attended with coughs."* Swarms of June bugs became an irritation, along with annoying buffalo gnats that clustered around the travelers' eyes and ears. As the train made its slow way across today's state of Kansas and along Nebraska's Platte River, the oxen became exhausted from pulling the wagons through the sand

LANDMARK LEGEND

1. Courthouse Rock
2. Chimney Rock
3. Scotts Bluff
4. Independence Rock
5. Devil's Gate
6. South Pass
7. Soda Springs
8. City of Rocks
9. The Whitman Mission
10. The Dalles

and mud. But the group pressed on, reaching Fort Laramie and then South Pass in early July.

Coffey had deep compassion for the oxen he drove and was troubled when others failed to care for their teams properly. Some of the animals died from exhaustion, but Coffey nurtured Bassett's oxen, especially if they showed signs of weakness. Many pioneer diaries noted that traveling the overland trails revealed hidden character strengths and weaknesses, since the demanding conditions tested the overlanders' patience, integrity, and empathy. Coffey's concern for the animals illustrates what must have been a gentle nature.

After being on the trail for two months, the travelers were sick and worn out, but they knew that delays would be disastrous. They pushed ahead, finishing their trek across present-day Wyoming and moving into southern Idaho while battling dust and relentless mosquitos. By late July, they approached the northeast corner of today's Nevada on the California Trail, and the following week reached the Humboldt River.

Coffey's wagon train lost more members than it picked up along the way and eventually dwindled to a handful. Even so, thick dust roiled behind the wheels. Israel Hale said: *"How our cattle stand it I am unable to say, for it is often the case that we cannot see oxen or wagon for the dust. . . ."* The grass was so dry that it broke if stepped on, and the emigrants had to build campfires with sagebrush.

Hoping to avoid the arid Humboldt Sink and the Forty Mile Desert, the travelers decided to turn onto the Applegate Trail in today's northwestern Nevada, thinking it was a faster route. It was late August and thoughts of winter influenced their choice. But the Applegate, which traversed vast, parched landscapes of its own, offered only sparse water sources. Coffey's party began to regret the decision. As the blazing sun beat down, the trail turned to sand, making it even harder for the oxen to haul the wagons. Sometimes traveling at night while burning greasewood stalks for light, the group labored from spring to spring, searching desperately for feed and water.

Coffey recalled that the final miles to Black Rock Springs, a thermal water source in Nevada's high desert about fifty miles from the Humboldt, was a life-or-death push for the animals. Dead cattle from earlier wagon trains fouled the trail. This dismal sight, the terrible stench, and poor drinking water made the long day almost intolerable. Coffey knew the look of dehydrated oxen. Their eyes seemed to shrink and turn dull, sinking deep into their orbits, and the animals became sluggish. Before reaching the springs, he doctored one of Bassett's failing oxen with rest and a precious reserve of water. Then, at the peak of the crisis, rare clouds suddenly blocked the blistering sun. Coffey reported in his reminiscence that a breeze sprang up and the animals seemed to revive. The dust blew away, and a few welcome raindrops fell. With the change in weather, the party reached the springs without losing cattle.

Coffey recollected that near one night's camp, a worn-out ox went down and was unable to get up. As it lay dying, the men could hear it bellowing pitifully in the darkness and realized that wolves were ripping off pieces of its flesh. Coffey tried to talk some of the other men into joining him to put the ox out of its misery. None would, so he took two double-barreled shotguns and went alone to where the animal suffered, mercifully killing it with one bullet. He reserved the extra shots in case the wolves attacked him, but the predators stayed away and Coffey returned to camp unharmed.

September arrived as the party reached the long-awaited mountains. Near the border of what is now California, they found plenty of grass for the oxen, fresh cold water, and firewood, along with much less dust. On September 3, after doubling the teams, they reached the summit of the pass through what would soon be named the Warner Mountains. Surrounded by crags and timbered slopes, they took time to appreciate the view. Then, still a long way from the goldfields, they descended to the alkaline waters of Goose Lake.

Coffey recalled that the group began to run out of food. Rations were short, and some of the men suffered from scurvy. The travelers were no longer sure how much farther it was to the settlements, but they pushed ahead and turned onto the Lassen Trail for the last long stretch.

In mid-September, the party stopped because William Bassett was too sick to travel. Coffey almost certainly took over the man's responsibilities and provided his care. It took six days for Bassett to regain enough strength to move on. The group headed for the Sacramento Valley over variable roads—sometimes easily passable, other times taxing for the weakening animals.

Finally, after more than five months on the trail, the wagon train crawled into the Sacramento Valley near today's Vina, California. After resting briefly, the group decided to split up. Some went south to Sacramento, while others turned north to dig for gold at Reading's Springs, which soon would become the boomtown of Shasta. Coffey and Bassett were among the smaller group who went north. By then, it was mid-October.

Mining for gold required immense physical labor. Despite being undernourished, Coffey was ready for the work, having wrestled Bassett's wagon over the unforgiving trail for more than 2,000 miles. At first, he and the other miners lived in a crude tent, but when the cold autumn rain and snow began to fall, they built a makeshift cabin for the winter. It is thought that William Bassett, still struggling with illness, could neither mine nor practice medicine at that point.

Coffey dug gold for Bassett, but determined to become a free man, he mined for himself in his off-hours. To build his savings, he cobbled shoes and did laundry for the other miners. He meticulously kept the gold he found for Bassett (which eventually totaled about $5,500) in one sack, and his own earnings (slightly more than $600) in a separate one. It was probably in the spring of 1850 when Bassett decided they both should leave Reading Springs and travel first to Fremont and then to Sacramento for unknown reasons. Before leaving, Bassett counted the gold in both sacks, and then, much to Coffey's anger and dismay, he swept Coffey's gold into his own bag. It was the last Coffey would see of his earnings.

In late 1850 or early 1851, Basset decided the two of them should return to Missouri. Historical sources say they may have traveled by boat, crossing the Isthmus of Panama and making their way to New Orleans. Coffey no longer trusted Bassett and worried that he would be sold away from his family on the auction block in Louisiana. But Bassett waited until they were back in Missouri before selling Coffey for $1,000 to a woman named Mary Tindall.

Still in the grip of slavery, Coffey reunited with his family at the Tindall place, where Mahala had most likely been enslaved since birth. Two more children, Alvin and Stephen, were born to them. Some of the Tindall family were supportive of Coffey's pursuit of freedom. He persuaded Nelson Tindall, a relative of Mary's, to let him return to California and again mine enough gold to purchase his freedom. In 1854, he started west a second time. His trail experience from the first overland journey proved valuable, and he hired himself out along the way. Other details of the journey are scarce, but historians know that he arrived in California as planned and began mining and doing hired work in the Shasta area.

After long months of labor, he had again earned the required amount to purchase his own freedom. He wrote to Nelson Tindall asking for his manumission papers. Tindall reportedly trusted Coffey so much that he sent the papers, dated July 24, 1856, and signed by Mary Tindall, without waiting for the money. Coffey gladly received them and sent the Tindalls his savings. He consulted a lawyer to make sure the documents were complete, accurate, and correct. They were. The text also gave a description of Coffey's physical appearance, noting that he was about five feet ten inches tall and approximately 180 pounds, with gray eyes, bushy hair, and a scar on one cheek.

Rejoicing in his new liberty, he began working to free Mahala and the children. By 1857, he had earned the price of their freedom. Coffey later reported the amount to be about $2,500 total; other sources differ. Then he returned to Missouri to claim his family and take them to northern California.

Coffey and Mahala arranged for some of their children to live temporarily with their grandmother in Canada, while the remainder of the family migrated to Shasta County. There they settled into life as free citizens. Coffey supported his family by mining and cobbling shoes. He was also involved in an effort to make sure his children could attend school. A 1901 article from the Oakland Office of the *San Francisco Call* noted that Coffey helped pass a California law ensuring the formation of a special school district for offspring of Black Americans.

In 1860, he and Mahala brought their remaining children from Canada to join the rest of the family. Three more babies (Charles, Sarah, and Ora Fino) were born as free citizens between 1858 and 1862, bringing the total to eight living children. After years of upheaval, disappointment, and hard work, Coffey and Mahala must have rejoiced to have their whole family free and finally together under one roof. School was a part of their sons' and daughters' lives. Some sources indicate that it was held in the family home.

The 1870 census reported that Coffey was working as a teamster, using the experience he had gained on the overland trails. In 1871, the family moved to Tehama County near today's city of Red Bluff, where Coffey obtained a parcel of land. He and Mahala grew hay and raised turkeys. At one point, he took part in the Modoc War, providing teams to the U.S. Army. One by one, the children (all but Sarah, who died at the age of fifteen of an unknown cause) grew up and left home to start families of their own. Some reportedly took up homesteading like their parents. Coffey joined the Society of California Pioneers, a select group of settlers who had come to the state in its earliest days. He was the only Black American member, and he belonged to the elite group for the rest of his life.

Coffey and his "pretty Mahala," as he called her, enjoyed their last years together. Perhaps they sometimes sat quietly watching the California sun set on their farmland, talking over their lives and the lasting effect that liberty would have on the children they loved.

Mahala died in 1891, and Coffey, bereft and alone, moved away from the farm, probably to be near one of his seven living children. He donated a sum of money toward the construction of the Home for the Aged and Infirm near Oakland in Alameda County and lived there for three years at the end of his life.

Coffey died in 1902 at about eighty years old. In a statement prepared by the Society of California Pioneers, who attended his funeral as a group, he was described as *"perfectly honest"* and *"a noble man, ever generous to his unfortunate neighbor."*

Alvin Aaron Coffey had an unwavering vision of freedom for himself and his family. Resisting the almost universal racial prejudice prevalent in his day, he persevered. With hard work and strength of character, he set his family free and lived a life of compassion and generosity, surrounded by loved ones, friends, and the California land that helped make his vision come true.

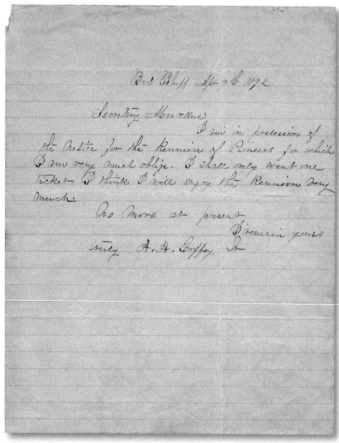

This handwritten note from Alvin Aaron Coffey to the Society of California Pioneers confirmed his attendance at a reunion. Dated April 9, 1892. COURTESY OF THE SOCIETY OF CALIFORNIA PIONEERS.

TROUBLE
IN DEATH VALLEY

The Story of William Lewis Manly

WILLIAM LEWIS MANLY FELT as if a heavy burden rested on his tired shoulders. His wagon party was depending on him to scout the best route through this unknown country, but he had only bad news to tell them. From where he stood alone on this barren mountaintop, he saw that crossing the daunting desert below was a death sentence. His friends, who were traveling with their spouses and small children, would never make it to the California settlements. They would surely parch, starve, or be stranded before that.

The long miles of this arid region, known today as Death Valley, stretched out before him, with no sign of desperately needed water. There was no speck of green for the starving oxen. Turning back was unthinkable; they had come too far through dangerous country for that. At first, this cutoff had seemed like a feasible shortcut to the California goldfields. Now, its uncharted, treacherous deserts and stony mountain ranges had become a terrible nightmare.

Manly, twenty-nine, had spent part of his boyhood in Jackson County, Michigan, where he helped his family build a log cabin and cultivate freshly broken land. Raised in a happy household, he learned to hunt and fish. At the age of twenty, he set out for Wisconsin Territory, supporting himself as a logger, miner, and trapper. He returned home occasionally, but during the winter of 1848–1849, news of gold discoveries in California reached him and he decided to make the long journey. By then, he was a capable, seasoned traveler with the necessary skills to undertake the trip. He had met a family with whom he planned to travel: Asabel Bennett, his wife Sarah Ann Dilley Bennett, and their three young children.

When the time came to rendezvous with the Bennetts, though, a miscommunication ruined their plans. Bennett had loaded Manly's best gun, ammunition, and buckskin clothing into his covered wagon as planned, but the two were unable to locate each other. Each started west separately. Manly joined another small wagon train and was hired to drive one of the teams.

His group followed the muddy track from St. Joseph, Missouri, to the California Trail. Manly wrote in his later account, *Death Valley in '49:*

William Lewis Manly, pictured later in his life. COURTESY, HISTORY SAN JOSÉ.

The Autobiography of a Pioneer, that he learned to handle the balky team by treating them kindly. He was concerned about the small size of the wagon train as they wound their way up the Platte River. Travel was slow and ponderous. Manly kept a diary, which later was lost.

Somewhere past Fort Laramie, the party fell in with a group of U. S. soldiers bound for Oregon, which increased their numbers and offered protection. The soldiers warned them that they had started out too late to expect to cross the Sierra Nevada before snowfall and would need to winter in Salt Lake City. Manly and the other drivers would lose their employment.

By then, the wagon train had crossed the Sweetwater River and reached South Pass. The snow on the mountains reminded them every day of their predicament. The idea of wintering in Salt Lake with little money and no jobs weighed heavily on the drivers. Finding employment in the settlement was unlikely. As they drove through the dry sagebrush country, they thought about what to do.

Reaching the beautiful, swift Green River, seven of the drivers came up with a plan: They would let the wagon owners handle their own teams and strike out on their own.

Coming across a small, half-buried ferryboat on the riverbank, they decided to use it to float down the Green. This, they were told, was a route to the Pacific Ocean. The river's course and conditions were mostly unknown, but it was a risk Manly and his companions were willing to take. Resurrecting the boat, they set out with their guns, some ropes, oars, hatchets, and a few provisions. Manly was named captain, being the most experienced traveler. For a few days, they journeyed quickly, averaging about thirty miles a day and hunting game to supplement their provisions.

Then the navigation became dangerous. Manly later reported in his autobiography that they had to unload the boat and tow, push, or pole it around massive boulders in the rushing current. In one bad spot, it wedged against a huge rock where it couldn't be budged.

The travelers were forced to abandon it.

Undaunted, the men made three hand-hewn canoes from nearby pines— a laborious process—and set off again, traveling swiftly. Manly was in charge of the largest boat, which held the provisions and ammunition. Before long the river again became treacherous and they had to portage their heavy canoes. In dangerous rapids, one of the seven men nearly drowned and most of their guns were washed downriver.

The winding Green River took them into today's state of Utah, where the once-abundant game dwindled. The men were facing hunger when they encountered a band of native people. Their chief, Wakara, whom Manly called Chief Walker, was a diplomat and leader of the Timpanogos Ute Nation. He communicated with Manly in sign language about the river, drawing a detailed map in the sand. Their present course, he indicated, would lead to a canyon where the stream was not navigable—a place they would not be able to escape, where food was scarce and death was likely. He advised them to go directly to Salt Lake. The chief showed them the route, pointing out hazards along the way, and gave them two horses in exchange for some extra clothing.

Manly took his advice. Two of the boaters decided to continue down the Green by canoe, but the others joined Manly. Loading their supplies onto the horses, the party of five set out on foot for Salt Lake. The overland route was exactly as Chief Wakara had described. Manly later wrote about his gratitude to the chief, crediting him with saving their lives.

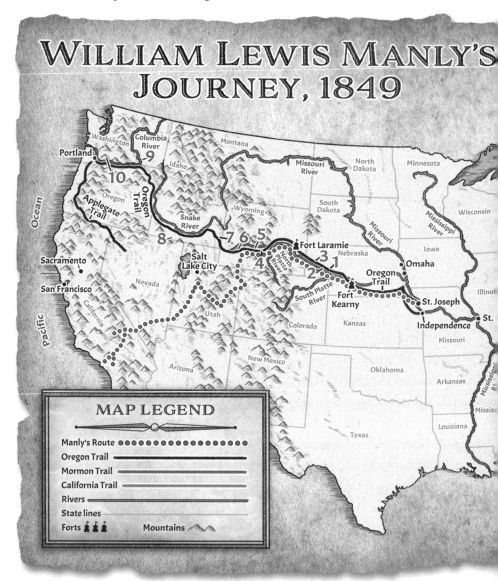

WILLIAM LEWIS MANLY'S JOURNEY, 1849

MAP LEGEND

Manly's Route •••••••••••••••••
Oregon Trail ————————
Mormon Trail ————————
California Trail ————————
Rivers ————————
State lines ————
Forts 🛖🛖🛖   Mountains ⛰⛰

About sixty miles south of the settlement, the men encountered a small wagon train that had stopped to camp. As the soldiers had indicated, it was too late in the season for them to cross the Sierra Nevada. Instead, they would wait for the October weather to cool, then head south through the desert to merge with the Old Spanish Trail, which led to Los Angeles. Manly and his companions decided to hire on and travel with the group.

Some of Manly's party found work to pay for their board. The others were invited to join the train as long as they could provide their own flour and bacon. Since the men had none, Manly and one of his companions started for Salt Lake to purchase the needed provisions. Along the way, they came across another wagon train, also camped and waiting until they could cross the desert ahead.

As the two men approached, a familiar-looking woman appeared. It was Sarah Bennett. Her husband was nearby. Manly, astounded to find the friends with whom he had originally planned to travel, joyfully greeted them. They still had his belongings packed away in their wagon. Bennett asked Manly to finish the journey with them, and Manly gladly agreed. His job would be to hunt game for the group. But he felt responsible for the Green River men, so he purchased their provisions and sent them back with his companion.

The Bennetts had two wagons, two drivers, and four teams of strong oxen. They and their companions soon joined other

LANDMARK LEGEND

1. Courthouse Rock
2. Chimney Rock
3. Scotts Bluff
4. Independence Rock
5. Devil's Gate

6. South Pass
7. Soda Springs
8. City of Rocks
9. The Whitman Mission
10. The Dalles

parties to form a large train of more than one hundred wagons. The new group elected a captain and established a formal written agreement. They, too, would follow the Old Spanish Trail.

Shortly after they started out, another group of wagon travelers overtook them. They had with them a convincing map of a cutoff that was much shorter than the Old Spanish Trail. After much discussion and debate, many of the emigrants decided to take the new shortcut. Bennett and Manly were among them. So were Manly's friend, John Haney Rogers, who had joined them from the Green River group, and one of Bennett's acquaintances named J. B. Arcan (or Arcane). There was also a party of spirited young gold seekers who called themselves the Jayhawkers.

It was November 4, 1849.

Asabel and Sarah Bennett had three young children: George, age seven; Melissa, four; and Martha Ann, not quite two. Arcan and his wife, Abigail, had one child, Charles, about three years old. Some historical accounts say that Abigail was pregnant.

Their route, already arid, worsened as they set out over the Great Basin Desert, a landscape never before traveled by wagons. After a few days they came to a wide, impassable abyss. When the first scouts reported there was no way to cross, many of the travelers turned back. Eventually a way across the gap was discovered and the new, smaller group (about twenty-seven wagons, according to Manly) pressed ahead, convinced they were taking a better, shorter course. Little did they know that their path through today's southern Utah and Nevada headed straight to what is now called Death Valley and the vast, deadly mountains surrounding it.

The travelers split into smaller and smaller groups as they desperately tried to work their way across the unforgiving landscape. The Jayhawkers took off at a faster pace. Manly and Rogers stayed with Bennett and Arcan.

Days of hard travel turned into weeks. Sources of water became fewer. Manly and twenty-seven-year-old John Rogers scouted ahead. Both men were skilled lookouts and excellent marksmen, but food began running out. The two split up to maximize their chances of finding game and water, but the game was gone and water was nearly impossible to find.

Manly's autobiography described his desperation and sense of responsibility. He thought about setting off on his own for California, confident he could get himself out of the trouble they were in. But the Bennetts were his friends. To desert them and the others was out of the question. (". . . *I felt I should be morally guilty of murder . . .*" he wrote.) So, day after day, he tramped through the desiccated terrain, climbing every butte, searching. Their party numbered only seven wagons by then.

"*It is not in my power to tell how much I suffered in my lonely trips, lasting sometimes days and nights that I might give the best advice to those of my party,*" he said. Occasionally he found a damp spot or a trickle of water. Once he was able to shoot a rabbit to take to his friends.

But he had only bad news about the route.

As he stood on his viewpoint gazing through the looking glass he had borrowed from J.B. Arcan, Manly saw today's Death Valley stretching for miles below him. The waterless expanse and the steep wall of mountains on the far side gave him little hope. He suspected there was no water for the next hundred miles—and it could be much farther than that to the settlements.

Manly saw evidence that the native peoples survived in this extreme environment and he took clues from their methods. But he had such foreboding for his own party that he privately wept at their prospects.

Back at the wagons, the children cried for a drink. Spirits were low. Energy was flagging. The animals hauling the heavy wagons were emaciated and parched. No rain had fallen, and shallow lakes had dried into white salt flats. The emigrants began killing their oxen for food.

There was no choice but to push on. The group descended toward the valley, encountering only brackish, undrinkable water. Even the downgrade was difficult for the weak animals. The travelers hoped for a pass through the desolate barrier of mountains, but saw none. Although it was December, the valley's daytime temperatures were uncomfortably hot.

Occasionally, a glimmer of good fortune showed itself. One cold night, snow fell, providing moisture for both the emigrants and their animals. Another time, the group came across a warm spring miraculously flowing from the ground. They stopped to refresh themselves and the oxen, filled their water vessels, and pointed the wagons to the mountains.

The Jayhawkers had made tracks in the sand. Following them through the rabbitbrush and wild creosote, Manly caught up with them. He found the young men smoking the meat from their weakest animals, using their wagons as fuel. Their once-spirited outlook had turned to grim desperation as they prepared to cross the mountains on foot.

Some of the men from Bennett's group also decided to go ahead on foot. Manly felt their chances were poor—everyone's chances were poor—but respected their decision. He, too, wanted to hurry on, but he refused to abandon the Bennetts and Arcans—especially the children and their distraught mothers. He led the wagons south along the base of the inhospitable mountains, today known as the Panamint Range, searching for a pass. Thinking the rugged Panamints were the Sierra Nevada, the party felt certain that the green valleys of California were on the other side.

Provisions were nearly gone, all but a few scraps of bread that they saved for the children. The stringy meat from the weakest oxen was the only other sustenance. After trying and failing to ascend a wild canyon that led from Death Valley into the Panamints, the party stopped, defeated, and wearily decided on a new plan. They would return to a seeping spring they had found earlier and stay there, while Manly and Rogers pushed ahead on foot to the settlements for help.

The two men set out. They carried as much food as the emigrants could spare and wore new rawhide moccasins on their feet. The group estimated that the men would return in about fifteen days. No one knew that the settlements were still about 250 miles away, an almost impossible trek over harsh mountains and through the Mojave Desert.

Both men were young and strong, but weeks of hard travel without adequate food and water had worn them down. Still, they hiked quickly, knowing the survival of the wagon travelers was at stake. Eleven adults and four children awaited their return, and they could last only as long as they had oxen to kill for food. The oxen were running out.

Manly and Rogers reached a new viewpoint that revealed long, waterless plains which would take days to cross, and at least two more mountain ranges, black and rocky in the distance. Already, they struggled to find water. When they did, it was briny or poisoned with alkali. They discovered that the Jayhawkers had taken the same route, and followed the party's footprints, hoping the group had discovered a spring. Finding none, Manly and Rogers began to suffer from extreme thirst. Their search for water became all-consuming as they struggled through the first range of mountains. Both sucked on small stones to encourage moisture in their mouths, but their saliva had dried up.

Their thirst was compounded by hunger and weakness, because without saliva they couldn't swallow the dried beef they carried. Manly used words like "despair" and "distress" in his account and he worried about survival. They split up, promising to fire their guns if one of them located water. That early morning, Manly was profoundly grateful to hear Rogers's gun; his partner had found a tiny patch of ice. They immediately put some in their mouths and melted the rest to drink. Somewhat refreshed, they kept on.

Miles of rough hiking brought them to a small camp of Jayhawkers, who had killed another ox near a slight waterhole. Sharing their meat and water, the Jayhawkers also passed on what little glum route information they knew. Manly and Rogers set out in the morning, and by nightfall they reached a second group of Jayhawkers. Some of the men who had left the Bennett party on foot were with them, out of food and in poor condition. Two others had died of thirst and starvation. Manly and Rogers shared what they had, even though there was no way to replenish it. Ahead was a vast, dry plain. Filling their canteens to the brim, the two hurried on, feeling as though they were staring death in the face.

A few miles later, they came across an unexpected spring where they drank and refilled their canteens. Ahead lay more mountains. Seven days had passed, and Manly knew they could not possibly return to the stranded emigrants in the allotted fifteen days. There was nothing to do but go on. Yucca began to dot the landscape, a curiosity which Manly noted in his autobiography.

Finally reaching the snowy mountains, they searched for a trail and found one. As they climbed, a crow appeared, then a hawk, and then a quail, all of which they shot for their supper. They reached the snow and tramped over the pass on its hardened surface. As they descended, they came across a bubbling brook of the purest, most delicious water they had tasted for months. Drinking their fill and enjoying their meal, the men were revitalized. Soon they were trekking through shady oaks and cottonwoods.

Suddenly, Manly felt a piercing pain in his left knee. As he hobbled after Rogers, it grew worse until he could barely walk. The two kept on at a slower pace. Manly worried that his injury would hinder their ability to rescue their friends, so he told Rogers to leave him behind. Rogers refused. Before long, they came across horses in a field and then the remains of an old mine. Finally, from a nearby hilltop, they looked down on a grassy meadow dotted with oaks and a huge herd of cattle. Rejoicing, they knew they had reached civilization.

Still desperately hungry, they shot a young steer, ate their fill, and refilled their knapsacks with the jerked meat. Both recognized their theft but were too close to starvation to forego the food. At long last, as December faded into January 1850, they encountered a few settlers and campers who pointed them to the *Rancho San Francisquito* near the old San Fernando Mission and today's city of Santa Clarita.

Although the settlers spoke only Spanish, the two men managed to describe their situation. The settlers invited them to eat and sleep, then provided supplies, provisions, and two packhorses for their rescue efforts. One woman gave them four sweet oranges, one for each child waiting for help.

As the men set off on the long, difficult return journey, they were able to buy another horse and a sturdy mule from a wagon party they met. Now they could ride, which increased their speed and let Manly rest his hurt knee.

Days passed, but as the landscape got harsher, the horses began to fail. Manly and Rogers buried some of their relief provisions and grieved when they had to abandon the animals near a steep, dry cliff in their path which they named "the waterfall." The little mule was skilled at traveling in the desert and nimbly carried supplies up the jagged, rocky ledge.

As the men retraced their route on foot, they knew where to find trickles of water, and they had food to sustain them. The mule ably fended for herself. Manly's knee improved, but their trip was taking twice as long as anticipated. They worried that their friends were dead of thirst or starvation or had given up on waiting and tried to go on, a decision that would have been fatal.

Finally, twenty-six days after they set out, the footsore men spotted the stranded wagons. Only four of the seven they'd left remained, and those were missing their canvas covers. There was no sign of life. They fired a shot to announce their arrival and watched closely. One by one the Bennetts and Arcans crawled out from under the wagons, haggard but alive. All of the others had gone on.

The families, overcome with relief, welcomed Manly and Rogers with heartfelt embraces and tears. Sarah Bennett had been sure the children would perish; little Martha was dangerously close to dying. After they shared a meal, the group peppered their rescuers with questions: What was the route like? Why had the two been gone so long? Must they leave the wagons behind?

Manly and Rogers were clear but encouraging. The settlements were much farther than they had thought, the men reported, but now they knew the route and where the waterholes were. The wagons must be abandoned, while the party's few remaining oxen would be brought along. It might be difficult to get them down the dry "waterfall," but the men thought it could be done.

The wagon travelers told Manly and Rogers that when the two hadn't returned after the allotted time, the group had reluctantly decided to leave the wagons and try to keep going. They had begun making harnesses and slings from the canvas wagon covers for the oxen, enabling the animals to carry the children and some supplies. Manly, who described himself as *"handy with the needle,"* helped the women finish the job, working beneath the wagons to avoid the baking sun. By then, it was about February 1, 1850.

Bennett's gentlest ox, Old Crump, was chosen to haul the two youngest children in the slings, while the older two rode on his back. Abigail Arcan, determined to save a cherished piece of her family heritage, is said to have worn a handwoven tablecloth as a shawl.

The party set out across the parched landscape.

Their journey got off to a slow start. The oxen, unaccustomed to hauling loads on their backs, bucked and thrashed until they were subdued enough to carry their cargo. Manly and Rogers led the way, retracing their steps again. When the group reached the "waterfall," they urged the reluctant animals over the cliff onto a soft bed of sand the men had piled up below. The oxen landed without serious injury. The smart, resilient mule had less trouble, landing securely on her feet.

Day after day, the men guided the exhausted party from waterhole to waterhole. The sharp, broken stones underfoot shredded their moccasins until their feet were bloody and raw. Their clothing was ripped and tattered. Little Charles Arcan developed a ferocious rash all over his body.

Manly and Rogers kept up an encouraging banter. The two sometimes went ahead to set up camp and prepare food. They found the provisions they had buried earlier. When those were gone, they began killing the oxen again for sustenance. The hides were used to make new moccasins for everyone. This included the remaining animals, whose hooves were sore from the knifelike rocks.

To stop for long would have been fatal. Manly and Rogers urged the party over boulders, through prickly desert greasewood, along salt flats devoid of grass or water, and over baking sand. One night, an unexpected storm left the travelers wet and cold. Arcan began carrying his son, whose rash chafed painfully in Old Crump's sling. That unbalanced the load, so Bennett carried little Martha. The party struggled along, worn out and miserable.

Slowly, their situation improved.

First, they came upon yucca and snow in the mountains, and then wild birds. Joyfully, the group stopped at the same crystal-clear stream their guides had found earlier and drank eagerly. Manly followed some faint animal tracks and managed to provide a supply of meat. Charles Arcan and Martha Bennett began to improve. Their gaunt, worn-out parents felt some strength return.

The travelers soon reached the green valleys they had sought for so long. Elated, they rested in grassy meadows and camped under spreading oaks, eating their fill and drinking the sweet water. Finally, they approached the settlements. Their agonizing escape from Death Valley had taken twenty-three days.

The kind Spanish-speaking woman who had sent the oranges to the children met them. Soon the hospitable settlers at the *Rancho San Francisquito* had fed and sheltered the straggling group. They were about thirty miles from Los Angeles.

The party split up there, with tears of gratitude toward the rescuers. The Arcans started on horseback for San Francisco and the Pacific coast while the others went on to Los Angeles. They could not stop rejoicing about their survival and the rich, beautiful land that now surrounded them. Manly noted in his account that they had been on the road for a year. The "shortcut" to California had robbed them of more than four months.

Asabel and Sarah Bennett met some acquaintances who clothed and fed them until they could all go north to the goldfields. Manly chanced upon James and Juliet Brier, another family of Death Valley emigrants who had also nearly perished on the cutoff. They had arrived in the settlements earlier and were running a boardinghouse. The Briers hired Manly to haul water for them, and invited him to stay.

As soon as he had recuperated and earned some money, Manly gratefully said goodbye to the Briers and started north to the goldfields. Along the way, he found the Bennetts again, and together they made their way to the Mariposa mines near today's Yosemite National Park. They learned how to pan for gold, but had no luck, so they continued north until they found viable claims northeast of Sacramento near Georgetown. There, Manly was able to mine *upward of two thousand dollars in gold.*

In November 1850, keeping his valuable ten-pound bundle close, he returned to Wisconsin by ship, crossing the Isthmus of Panama by hired boat and on foot. After traveling by steamer through Havana, New Orleans, and St. Louis, he took a riverboat almost to Peoria, Illinois. Then he finished the journey to Wisconsin by buying passage on a stagecoach, hiring a farm wagon, and walking. Disappointed in the opportunities there, he stayed only briefly before returning to California, arriving by sea in July 1851. He took up mining again, this time on the north fork of the Yuba River.

John Haney Rogers had also gone to the goldfields to try his hand at mining. He later moved to Merced, where he lived for the rest of his life. He and Manly remained close friends.

William Lewis Manly lived a long life in California. Historical sources state that he eventually purchased 250 acres of farmland on present-day Communications Hill in San Jose. In 1862, at age forty-two, he married Mary Jane Woods of Lodi. Their descendants owned and resided on the beautiful knoll for many years. Today, a street and a park there bear his name, as do several landmarks in Death Valley.

Manly died in 1903 near Lodi at the age of eighty-three. Honor and integrity had been the driving forces in his life. His rescue mission with John Rogers to save their friends has gone down in history as one of the most selfless deeds of the American West. It is for this inspirational feat that he is best remembered.

This map, drawn by William Lewis Manly, shows his party's route through Death Valley and beyond. He created it later in his life, possibly when publishing his autobiography in 1894. The map is oriented with north on the righthand side. PHOTOGRAPH COURTESY OF SCVHISTORY.COM.

INJURY AND ILLNESS
ON THE CALIFORNIA TRAIL

The Story of William Henry Hart

WILLIAM HENRY HART OF QUINCY, Illinois, made careful plans for his trip to the California gold country in 1852. In early February, he and three companions (Daniel Streeter, William C. Reed, and Thomas Russell) ordered a sturdy wagon to be built to their specifications. When it was ready, they stretched two layers of heavy canvas over the bows and began assembling their gear and supplies. Hart, twenty-three, bought a gun and an India rubber coat, along with blankets and durable clothing. The men added four oxen, a few cows, provisions, axes, kettles, a tar bucket to hold axle lubricant, and other necessities. On April 21, 1852, they departed for their California Trail jump-off spot on the Missouri River near Council Bluffs, Iowa. Hart kept a journal in which he recorded each day's events in even, flowing penmanship. It eventually became five small volumes.

In the beginning, their inexperience caused minor delays and mishaps, which the four of them laughed about as they traveled. A yoke of steers ran off in the direction of home, and William Reed followed in pursuit. But he was carrying all of his money in heavy coins in his pockets and was unable to keep up. Hart took over, sprinting on foot to get ahead of the animals and successfully turning them around.

Inside the wagon, the men had constructed a removable platform of loose boards, eight feet long and three feet wide. The boards served as a table for out-door meals, but when replaced in the wagon, they made a smooth, hard sleeping surface. Early in the trip, Hart described how difficult it was to sleep with all four men crowded onto this narrow space. They had to lie head-to-toe like wedges, each wrapped in his own blankets. Hart was glad for the strong morning coffee, which invigorated him after the first sleepless night. He also noted that bacon, which he had always disliked, tasted delicious when one was ravenous.

Spring rain followed them, and the four soon made a rule about climbing into the wagon with muddy boots on. Dirt must have gotten into a few of their meals,

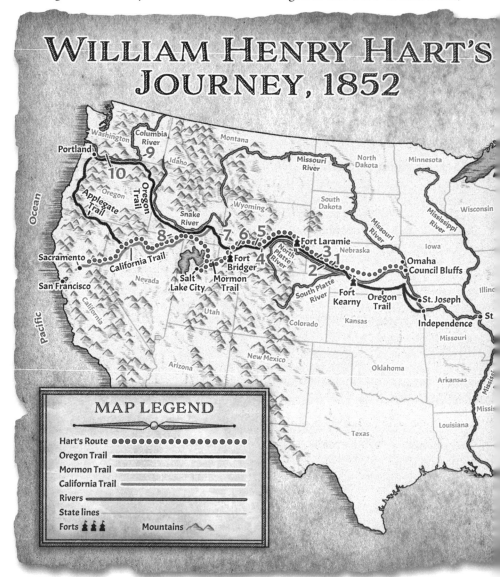

WILLIAM HENRY HART'S JOURNEY, 1852

MAP LEGEND

Hart's Route ●●●●●●●●●●●●●●●●●●
Oregon Trail
Mormon Trail
California Trail
Rivers
State lines
Forts 🏠🏠🏠   Mountains ⌃⌃

because Hart commented that the new rule was to *"keep the mud and dirt from mixing too freely with our provisions."* They took turns cooking. Hart knew he was inept at making even simple meals, but with Daniel Streeter's help, he learned how to stew meat and fry bacon. He had trouble figuring out how much saleratus (a leavening agent) to add to pancake dough, but soon became expert at making coffee.

The men had plenty of cooking disasters. Sometimes the sticks suspending a pot over the campfire burned through, dumping their meal into the flames. Other times, they burned their food in the intense heat of the fire. With practice, these things happened less often, especially after they found some iron rods discarded along the trail, picked them up, and used them to support their pots over the fire.

At one river crossing, Hart rode in the wagon, holding on to the guns they had placed on top of the load in case they needed them. When the wagon lurched down the steep streambank, the load shifted and one of the guns fired, setting Thomas Russell's bedding on fire and destroying it. Hart's diary didn't mention what Russell used for covers after that, but he may have adopted the saddle blankets that had escaped damage.

When the four reached the Missouri River in mid-May, they happened to find a small company of wagon travelers from back home and joined them. One of seven wagons, they crossed the wide river on a ferry. Before long, they merged with a second company, and their wagons totaled nineteen. The group elected a captain and

LANDMARK LEGEND

1. Courthouse Rock
2. Chimney Rock
3. Scotts Bluff
4. Independence Rock
5. Devil's Gate
6. South Pass
7. Soda Springs
8. City of Rocks
9. The Whitman Mission
10. The Dalles

organized guard duty. Hart, like many other emigrants, found standing guard the most difficult task of the journey. He disliked tending cattle in the dark and found it more exhausting than the strenuous daytime travel.

As they journeyed up the north bank of the shallow Platte River in today's state of Nebraska, Hart wrote that he suspected drinking standing water without boiling it caused illness. In a year when deadly waterborne cholera was rampant on the overland trails, this belief may have saved his life; others in the train died abruptly of the terrible disease.

Eight of the wagons separated from the train just beyond the junction of the Loup and Platte Rivers, and went on by themselves. Their reduced number meant that Hart drew guard duty more often, but he noted that they were *"well satisfied with the division."* His diary gave no reason for the split.

On the Platte River in mid-June, the men threw away their raingear—India rubber coats and oilcloth—thinking that there would be no more rain until they reached California. They undoubtedly got drenched as the violent summer thunderstorms continued.

A funeral stopped the train on June 6. Mrs. Emery, one of the wagon train's few women, had fallen ill with cholera. Her death happened swiftly, and her fellow travelers held an emotional funeral and burial. Hart was deeply affected by the event. In his journal, he described the day in detail, from the handcrafted coffin and grave marker to the sad procession of emigrants who laid the woman to rest. A few days later, another member of the wagon train, John Hughes, died and was buried with the same compassion.

When the group reached Fort Laramie, Hart and his friends hoped to replenish their coffee and sugar, but were disappointed to learn that coffee was selling for an exorbitant fifty cents a pound. Sugar was worse at a dollar. They strictly limited their purchases, deciding to depend on the dwindling supplies they had brought from home.

In late June, the party left the relatively flat road along the Platte and entered the Laramie Mountains. The trail turned bad, marked by steep hills, rocks, and sharp bends. On June 22, while helping maneuver the load down an abrupt descent, Hart reported that the *"lock chain became loosened,"* and the wagon began hurtling toward the bottom, putting him and the oxen in danger. When he tried to grab one of the ironclad wheels to slow it down, the wagon ran over his big toe, crushing it. The pain was searing. A foot injury could be fatal on the overland trails. Infection could set in, or, at the very least, the resulting disability could keep a traveler from doing the constant work needed to complete the journey. Hart had good reason to be worried. With nothing but a homemade cornmeal poultice to dull the pain, he endured several days with such a severe, throbbing ache that he had to ride in the wagon.

As he jolted along under the canvas cover for the next eighty miles, terrible thoughts must have run through his mind. He desperately disliked not being able to pull his weight with the never-ending chores, and he probably worried that his foot might not heal correctly. Someone gave him a primitive crutch so he could hobble around camp and help with the work.

As the days passed, his agony slowly diminished. Several nights later, Hart reported being able to help guard the cattle, which suggested that the wound was healing. Bit by bit, he gratefully resumed his activities.

On July 2, he and two friends climbed to the top of the precipice forming one side of Devil's Gate. After taking in the spectacular vista and listening to the Sweetwater River rushing by below, Hart wrote that he would remember that day of traversing the nearly perpendicular cliffs as the *"most thrilling adventure of my life."*

The wagon train detoured to a grassy meadow to celebrate the Fourth of July. Everyone pitched in to prepare a grand celebration complete with a makeshift flag, a long dinner table protected from the wind by an awning and blankets, wildflower decorations, and a feast of antelope and prairie fowl. After the meal, the travelers drank brandy and enjoyed an improvised parade, a ballgame, and a noisy gun salute. Hart drank water, foregoing the brandy.

While heading up the Sweetwater, he bought a pair of moccasins from the Shoshone people who approached to trade and found the leather shoes very comfortable unless the ground was rocky. The wagon train inched closer to South Pass. Nights were cold at the higher elevation as the beautiful Wind River Mountains came into view. Even though it was July, snowbanks were scattered along the road. The trail was rocky; it wore down the oxen's hooves until they limped in pain. Hart and his companions fashioned footwear for the animals, tacking pieces of leather onto each hoof or crafting rawhide moccasins that tied around their fetlocks.

Near the Green River in today's state of Wyoming, several of the wagons split off for Oregon after a rousing goodbye from the rest of the party. Hart's group pressed on to California. In mid-July, as they neared Fort Bridger, Hart fell ill with body pain and a headache. He suspected mountain fever. Again, he had to ride in the wagon, too sick to walk, although he tried to help with the unrelenting trail tasks. Nearly a week later he wrote that the illness had left him with such dreadful fatigue that he could barely do his chores. He struggled for days as the wagons crept through the rugged Wasatch Mountains into what is now Utah. Seven miles from the settlement of Great Salt Lake City, they stopped to rest the cattle. Some of the emigrants attended a celebration in town, but Hart spent the day in the

A wagon train is shown navigating Echo Canyon, a difficult spot on the overland trail, as emigrants toiled through the Wasatch Range of the Rocky Mountains in today's state of Utah. PHOTOGRAPH COURTESY OF THE RARE BOOKS DIVISION, SPECIAL COLLECTIONS, J. WILLARD MARRIOTT LIBRARY, UNIVERSITY OF UTAH, RALPH CHAMBERLAIN PHOTOGRAPH COLLECTION, P0287, 201992.

shade under the wagon nibbling on dry crackers and "crawling to the creek for water." Nevertheless, he wrote in his journal that he thought he was improving.

Later, he was able to make it into the settlement. He described at length the city's wide streets and public buildings, which included an adobe courthouse and a Mormon tabernacle. One of Hart's original travel partners, William Reed, asked the others to buy him out; he had decided to stay in Salt Lake City until fall. The others agreed, purchasing his share of the outfit. Hart borrowed his portion of the money from Daniel Streeter, whom he later repaid.

The men spent part of a day buying hay and replenishing their flour and soap. They had the cattle shod with iron shoes; stock animals typically went through several pairs of shoes on the overland journey. Pressing on, they crossed the northern end of the Salt Lake Valley, leaving the mountains behind and continuing into the Great Basin, resting the cattle where good grass could be found. Hart was getting back on his feet and made no further mention of his illness.

In mid-August, the party reached the Humboldt River Valley. Instead of the dreary, insect-infested expanse along the river that other pioneers reported, Hart wrote that the Humboldt provided a pleasant and relatively easy stretch. That was in spite of the choking dust that covered the emigrants until they were, as he put it, *"hardly recognisable."*

Weary but determined, the travelers finally arrived at the Big Meadows, a wide, flat area of sloughs and marshes near the Humboldt Sink. It was September 4. There they laid in a supply of grass and water for the treacherous Forty Mile Desert crossing ahead.

Starting out on September 7, they were pleased to find that the road was good, thanks to favorable conditions that year. Although they ran into a long stretch of deep sand, they managed to traverse the baking, waterless miles in just twenty-five hours, traveling partly at night and making occasional stops to refresh the oxen. Relieved, they reached the Carson River at the far edge of the desert on September 8, enjoying its cool, clear waters and resting the cattle.

Several days later, they caught sight of the Sierra Nevada, noting that snow blanketed the high peaks. Hart and his companions were worried about crossing the mountains with their battered wagon, which by then needed repairs. The oxen were worn out. At a small settlement in the Carson River Valley, they decided to sell their outfit and purchase mules and horses for the difficult route ahead. Seven other men joined them. Hart and his companions said goodbye to those who wanted to keep their wagons and travel more slowly, and rode into the mountains on September 16. It turned out to be *"a much worse place than we had ever anticipated,"* Hart wrote. Laboring up the slopes, they reached the first summit, where they camped by a mountain lake with abundant grass for the tired horses and mules.

The next day, they began climbing toward a second summit, higher than the first. Again, the progress was slow, but they finally reached the top, traveling mostly on foot to preserve the animals. Expecting a sweeping vista of California, they were disappointed that wildfire smoke blurred the view from their vantage point of 9,000 feet. They ran into snow, but Hart reported that the temperature was mild. Starting down the other side, the group came upon a trading shack where they purchased beef for their supper. They roasted it on long sticks held over the campfire, since they had left most of their cooking gear behind with the wagons. The September nights were cold, so they slept close to each other and the fire.

Placerville, California (ca. 1849), was also known as Hangtown or Dry Diggins. It was near Sutter's Mill, where flecks of gold discovered in a streambed in 1848 started the Gold Rush. PHOTOGRAPH COURTESY OF THE CENTER FOR SACRAMENTO HISTORY, FRANK CHRISTY COLLECTION, 1998/722/3726.

As they neared Placerville and the surrounding gold camps, they found small outlying settlements. The men bought hay for the horses and mules, along with a few provisions for themselves. Hart and his two partners were pleasantly surprised when they encountered three old friends from home who had also sold their wagons and teams and pushed ahead on horseback. The group finished the journey together, bedraggled and tired, arriving in Placerville the evening of September 19, 1852.

Hart reported being satisfied with the overland trip. His companions disagreed, saying they would never undertake such an exhausting journey again. Hart thought they were disappointed because they had been expecting a pleasure trip instead of a taxing overland undertaking.

The men immediately purchased shovels and gold pans, replenished their provisions, and left for the South Fork of the American River forty miles away. They'd heard about gold there. For a few days, they prospected unsuccessfully until their food ran out; then they returned to Placerville. Hart, who was looking for steady employment, decided to leave the gold camps in favor of the city. Perhaps troubled by lack of money, he traveled through Sacramento to San Francisco,

Prospectors posed with their equipment at a miner's camp near Placerville during the California Gold Rush.
PHOTOGRAPH COURTESY OF THE LIBRARY OF CONGRESS, LC-DIG-DS-04487.

where he met with a man named George Graham (probably a relative), who lent him fifty dollars. He made his way back to Sacramento, searching for a job. Failing to find work, he returned to the gold camps as winter approached and the weather turned cold and wet. Rainstorms caused widespread flooding, then turned into hail and snow. There was mud everywhere.

Hart spent the year alternating between mining and searching for a job. He sold his gun and his faithful horse, but had to borrow more money to get by. The cost of food was high, he reported, and the yield from the diggings was meager. Although he joined acquaintances in several excavations, nothing amounted to a steady income. He did earn enough to repay the money he had borrowed. At times, he lived in a shelter built of brush, or a leaky tent. His parents sent money from their home in New York, and George Graham helped again by buying a small cabin near Hart's diggings and letting him stay there.

In October 1853, more than a year after he had arrived in California, Hart found a job as a clerk and salesman in the town of Napa. When that position petered out, he decided to go into business for himself, establishing a small store in 1855. At first, sales were good, but when others set up competing businesses, Hart's profits dwindled and he was forced to close down.

After four years in California, he was ready to leave for the East Coast, where much of his family lived. Life in California had been a series of highs and lows. He'd enjoyed traveling and exploring the settlements of Sacramento, Stockton, and San Francisco, but the goldfields and job prospects had been disappointing. In December of 1856, intending to travel to New York by sea, he bought passage on a steamer bound for Nicaragua. There, he crossed the Central American Isthmus by stage and riverboats. When he reached Nicaragua's east coast, Hart caught a ship for the Atlantic Seaboard. Finally, on January 24, 1857, he arrived in New York, where his relatives and friends welcomed him.

Eventually, Hart returned to Quincy, Illinois, and married. He and his wife Jennie had three children. He became a postmaster for many years while raising his family, and at one time sold insurance. Jennie believed her husband would have traveled more during his life if circumstances had permitted. Hart died suddenly in 1888 at the age of fifty-nine.

William Henry Hart's trip west was a small fraction of his life, but he always remembered his overland journey. Despite suffering a foot injury and lying sick with fever in the lurching covered wagon, his writings about the California Trail were steady and positive. His ability to make friends and his strong work ethic helped him outlast the hard realities of Gold-Rush California. Although the diggings didn't produce enough wealth to sustain him—and a steady job was hard to come by—Hart took full advantage of his chance to see the world. Returning home with his wanderlust and gold fever reasonably satisfied, he lived out his life in the Midwest, little suspecting that his writings would someday offer a valuable perspective to the history of the California Trail.

"IT RAINED LIKE HELL ALL NIGHT"

The Story of Dr. John Hudson Wayman

ICY RAIN PELTED A SMALL GROUP of travelers moving slowly with their wagon through a prairie hollow. Dr. John Hudson Wayman pulled his wet overcoat close and shivered. This 1852 overland trip to California had begun uneventfully, but only four days from the jump-off point at St. Joseph, Missouri, a storm had hit.

This photograph of Dr. John Hudson Wayman was taken in the mid-1860s, a few short years before his death in San Francisco at the age of forty-six. PORTRAIT OF JOHN HUDSON WAYMAN, JOHN HUDSON WAYMAN PAPERS, BANC PIC 1981.060, THE BANCROFT LIBRARY, UNIVERSITY OF CALIFORNIA, BERKELEY.

Wayman, thirty-two, often jotted cheerful entries in his small purplish-red leather journal, but this time he noted that *"it rained like Hell all night"* and was *"very cold."* Like many trail diarists, the doctor sometimes made brief, cryptic entries, but other times wrote long descriptions. His spelling was inventive, his handwriting bold and dark. Wayman's diary stands out due to its generally sunny perspective and for the way it illustrates a typical overland experience. Some fundamental information is missing, like the names of fellow travelers and exactly how many others journeyed with him. (It is thought that his party consisted of seven to ten men.) He also didn't explain his motive for leaving his home and medical practice in Indiana. Instead, he chronicled day-to-day travel on the trail.

Wayman, who was from a large Indiana family, had graduated from the medical school at Cincinnati College and received his license to practice in the spring of 1842. At the time, medical knowledge was limited, and treatments were primitive. Physicians on the overland trails were asked to address everything from broken bones to gunshot wounds, snake bites, and infections, along with deadly illnesses. Without knowing the causes of diseases like cholera or mountain fever or scurvy, cures often missed their mark. Mixtures containing mercury or opium were used as remedies, along with poultices, herbs, castor or cod liver oil, and shots of whiskey. Purging, sweating, and bloodletting were also common. Although there is no evidence to show which methods Wayman used in tending his patients, it is likely that he made use of some of these common treatments.

The Medical College of Ohio, 1835. John Hudson Wayman received his medical education at this prestigious institution in the early 1840s. PHOTOGRAPH COURTESY OF THE OHIO HISTORY CONNECTION, AL04141.

As the men stopped to wait out the deluge, Wayman may have looked over his small supply of medicines and remedies in case anyone in the party took a chill from the weather. Wet feet were thought to be a cause of illness, and all of the travelers had wet feet.

Anticipating a cold night in soaked bedding, he probably longed for the warm, dry home he had left behind. He was glad to be on the road, though. The

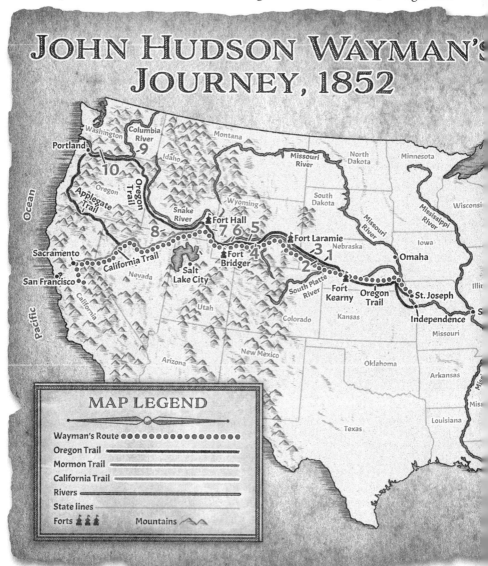

JOHN HUDSON WAYMAN'S
JOURNEY, 1852

MAP LEGEND

Wayman's Route ●●●●●●●●●●●●●●●
Oregon Trail
Mormon Trail
California Trail
Rivers
State lines
Forts 🏛🏛🏛   Mountains

past few years had been filled with grief. Family history suggests that the dark-haired, handsome doctor lost his young wife in 1849, and shortly afterward, his infant daughter. He was ready for a new start in California where opportunities seemed boundless. His older brother, James, also a physician, had already been to California but was disappointed and had decided to return home. Wayman was confident his own experience would be different.

When the storm subsided, the small party continued along the trail toward the Platte River and Fort Kearny. Their light wagon, pulled by sturdy oxen, carried their provisions and gear. Wayman described the *"sea of Prairie"* they crossed, which was intersected by deep streams with steep, muddy banks. Getting the wagon through was a constant challenge. Grass along the well-worn trail became as scarce as firewood, but there were graves everywhere. Cold temperatures, wind, and violent downpours plagued the men as they followed the Little Blue River and then the Platte to reach Fort Kearny on May 19.

LANDMARK LEGEND

1. Courthouse Rock   6. South Pass
2. Chimney Rock   7. Soda Springs
3. Scotts Bluff   8. City of Rocks
4. Independence Rock   9. The Whitman Mission
5. Devil's Gate   10. The Dalles

". . . it does me good to see even a respectable bush," Wayman wrote in frustration at the lack of wood for a campfire there. Two days later, having continued upstream, some of the men waded to an island and brought back kindling and logs for a fire. Wayman mentioned with satisfaction the hot bean soup they enjoyed.

Although dismayed by the barren terrain along the overland trail, he also recognized its stark beauty, noting that he felt inspired by the striking views. As the party wended its way toward the South Platte crossing, Wayman entertained himself by examining rocks and rock formations, especially in the river bluffs. He wrote knowledgeably about the specimens he found and gathered samples for a collection.

By the end of May, Wayman reported clear, warm days. When the group reached the famous Ash Hollow in present-day southwestern Nebraska, he noted that the area was a relief from the earlier monotonous landscape. Ash Hollow was an anticipated stopping place because it was scenic and lush with vegetation. Some pioneers described cool springs and a profusion of fragrant wild roses blooming there. Soon after, the party crossed the North Platte to travel along its less-used north bank, hoping that the sandy trail would improve and there would be better grazing for the animals. Prairie dog towns appeared. Wayman was fascinated by the endearing, black-eyed creatures. He took time to examine and classify one, comparing it with a gopher.

The month of June began with dry, sunny weather. Dust on the trail was becoming an issue, but Wayman took pleasure in seeing long-awaited landmarks: Courthouse Rock, Chimney Rock, and Scotts Bluff. He appreciated their unusual beauty and the vast distances surrounding them. At Scotts Bluff he added a sand-stone specimen to his collection.

Battling insects, the party pushed on into present-day Wyoming. There Wayman caught his first glimpse of the Rocky Mountains far in the distance. Thrilled, he wrote that they appeared *"Grand—Magnificent—Splendid."*

Fort Laramie was on the opposite bank of the North Platte. Wayman thought it was a cheerful sight—a bit of civilization in the midst of the wilderness. He crossed the river to mail a letter to his brother.

Before approaching the mountains, the trail crossed miles of dry terrain interspersed with poisonous alkali water and cacti. Sagebrush with woody stems became firewood, its pungent odor perfuming the air. Reaching the winding Sweetwater River, which flowed from the wild Wind River Range, the men stopped to enjoy its clear, fresh water. Wayman climbed nearby Independence Rock and reported on its composition. He enjoyed a day of rock hunting near Devil's Gate. At South Pass, the doctor admired the landscape, especially the snowcapped mountains in view. It was June 22. By embarking early on the trail and traveling lightly, the party had made good time.

They pressed ahead, crossing the Little Sandy and Big Sandy Rivers, but took a short detour on the Green River to bypass the many wagons waiting for the primitive ferry. In 1852, hordes of travelers were traversing the overland trails. Some of them described lines of wagons as far as they could see, both to the east and west. Competition was fierce, especially for scarce resources like firewood and grass. Trailside litter had reached hideous proportions, as hurried emigrants tossed out precious belongings to lighten their loads.

By the end of the month, the road had become more difficult. Heading into the mountains, the party crossed Ham's Fork in southwest Wyoming. There, Wayman reported green aspens, pines, and abundant wildflowers. He left his group for a morning horseback ride to attend a sick man from another company.

On June 30, the doctor wrote about illnesses he had witnessed along the trail, especially mountain fever. He noted that he had seen several cases. Historians speculate that mountain fever may have included a number of diseases not recognized at the time, especially Colorado tick fever and Rocky Mountain spotted fever, both caused by tick bites. Symptoms included severe headache, high fever, and rash. Survivors sometimes had long-term complications such as hearing loss or confusion. Mountain fever was common along the overland trails in spring and early summer when ticks were most active.

After eight weeks on the trail, the doctor may also have encountered cases of food poisoning, toothaches, and crushed fingers. Infected gashes and sprained or broken limbs were common, as was dysentery. Many wagon parties included a physician for their safety and peace of mind. Wayman's companions were no doubt grateful to have him along, armed as he was with medical knowledge and a kit of remedies.

It was early July when the group entered today's state of Idaho. Wayman, like other emigrants, was struck by the beautiful, fertile Bear River Valley as well as the unusual springs that bubbled carbonated water from the ground near present-day Soda Springs. The Fourth of July was cold, with a mountain snowstorm. Wayman purchased a warm buffalo robe and a shirt from the native people they encountered, and the party continued west, taking the Hudspeth Cutoff rather than the well-traveled road through Fort Hall. The doctor came across two ill men, whom he diagnosed and treated for possible cholera. As the group completed the shortcut, merged onto the main California Trail, and passed the City of Rocks, they were still making good time. They entered today's state of Nevada in mid-July.

The men followed the banks of the Humboldt River, usually covering twenty miles or more per day. Grass and wood were still scarce, but the pioneers could depend on the warm, murky Humboldt for water. Wayman reported that his party was in good health, including the cattle, mules, and horses. His diary entries focused on describing the countryside instead of the dull monotony that other Great Basin travelers deplored. But the days were long and hot. Dust on the primitive road got deep, then deeper. Suffocating clouds billowed up, making travel almost intolerable.

Wayman continued to collect rock samples for his collection, delighted with each find. A man of many interests, he found each new region unlike anything he had encountered in his life. In his diary, he wrote descriptions that would later remind him of the wonders he had seen.

Early in August, the group reached the Big Meadows at the lower end of the Humboldt River. There, like earlier travelers, they cut a supply of grass to carry with them into the long, difficult desert ahead. Wayman reported on the stark beauty of the area, but by then was weary of the seemingly endless Humboldt and was eager leave it behind. On August 4, they set out over the desolate Forty Mile Desert. Deep sand slowed their progress.

Wayman's party traveled all day and all night, with short breaks to feed the animals. They drank the water they carried with them. Relying on their own endurance and that of their animals, they crossed the desert without mishap. The men stopped briefly on the Carson River at the rough settlement of huts and tents where traders offered goods for sale, especially whiskey and, as Wayman put it, *"all kinds of vulgar amusements."*

The men found a nearby grove of leafy cottonwoods and willows and stopped over to rest. Then they moved on, following the Carson River toward the daunting

Sierra Nevada, the main obstacle between them and California. On August 10, Wayman mentioned that he backtracked fifteen miles to treat a sick man and woman. He camped overnight with the other company before catching up with his own.

In his absence, Wayman's party had decided to lay over for about ten days, when a team belonging to one of its members was due to arrive. It's unclear why this was important, but Wayman was impatient with the delay. For the next ten days, his diary reflects his feelings as the group stalled near Mormon Station, now Genoa, Nevada. The Sierra Nevada awaited nearby, and the doctor was eager to cross. Irritated by the stop, and then angry, he vented his frustration in his diary, cursing the situation and his fellow travelers.

Finally, on August 22, the group started up again. According to the guide-book they carried, the most difficult part of the trail was ahead. They entered the steep canyon leading to Carson Pass over *"the worst road that ever was traveled,"* wrote Wayman. He described the geology of the area and its sheer mountains, thick pines, and snow. Like many parties, they struggled and heaved their way over the route, but with just one wagon, their ascent was easier and faster than it was for others. They reached the rocky summit in late August. The road ahead was downhill.

On August 27, after descending the steep, timbered western slopes of the Sierra Nevada, Wayman and his party arrived in Placerville, a jumble of rough-hewn wooden buildings and log cabins carved out of the wilderness. The doctor was glad to be done with the overland trek. Two days later he continued to Sacramento, and then traveled by stagecoach to the new towns of Stockton and Sonora, searching for a good mining opportunity. He stayed the winter.

Wayman's diary entries dwindled, but later he wrote a letter to his brother James indicating that he journeyed home to Indiana in 1853 to visit his family. He returned to California in 1854, this time traveling by way of Panama. The doctor settled in Forest City, a prosperous mining town northeast of Sacramento, setting up a medical practice and investing part of his income in the mines.

Several years later, when the area began to decline, he moved to Carson City, Nevada Territory, near the site where the Comstock Lode had been discovered.

There he met a young widow, Margaret Ormsby, and the two were married in February 1863. Orion Clemens, brother of Samuel Clemens (Mark Twain), performed the ceremony. Historians speculate that the Waymans were acquainted with both men, who lived together in Carson City at the time.

The couple, along with Margaret's fourteen-year-old daughter, Lizzie, stayed in Carson City temporarily and then moved to San Francisco, where Wyman is thought to have continued his medical practice. Their time there was destined to be short. A little more than three years after she and the doctor were married, Margaret died in childbirth. Her death was a blow. Several months later, Wayman is believed to have contracted incurable tuberculosis. The terrible disease wreaked its havoc, and he died in January 1867 at the age of forty-six.

John Hudson Wayman had filled his short life to the brim. In just four and a half decades, he earned a medical education, married twice, became a widower twice, undertook two epic journeys to California by different routes, and became part of the Gold Rush. He worked at his medical practice, treating the settlers around him.

By keeping a diary of his overland trip, Wayman made his voice heard through the centuries. His wagon trip was remarkably free of accidents and disaster, but he endured his share of long, grueling days and cold nights. His account reflects his delight in new experiences and his appreciation for the beauty that surrounded him. A lively, inquisitive, and sometimes exasperated emigrant, Wayman brought his skills and aspirations to the far-flung mining towns of the American West. In his diary, he wrote: *"I am well pleased with this place. . . ."*

THE LOST WAGON
TRAIN OF 1853

The Story of Benjamin Franklin Owen

BENJAMIN FRANKLIN OWEN REINED IN his tired horse and peered over the precipice. These craggy Cascade Mountains seemed determined to prevent him and his companions from reaching the remote settlements in the far-off Willamette Valley. Impossible tangles of downed trees and thick undergrowth blocked the way ahead, and this cliff kept them from turning north. They could only go back the way they'd come, wasting more of their scant rations and precious time.

Despair overwhelmed him as he thought about the friends they'd left behind. Their wagon train was lost in this vast country, and food had nearly run out. No one, not even the guide, knew the exact route to the green Oregon valleys. Owen and several other men had offered to ride ahead to scout and bring back provisions for the families who were inching through the dreadful, dry landscape behind him, enduring terrible thirst and near starvation somewhere in Oregon Territory's high desert.

Frank Owen had started west with two friends, Joel B. Kistner and Christian H. Norman, on March 31, 1853, from Stoddard County, Missouri, bound for the goldfields. They traveled steadily through Missouri with their secondhand wagon, heading northwest toward the Oregon Trail. Owen sometimes rode his pony, Mack, and at night, the three young men camped at welcoming farmhouses along the route. Owen endured a bout of sickness, possibly cholera, early in the trip, but slowly recovered. By the time they had crossed present-day Kansas and then reached Fort Kearny along the Platte River, they had been traveling for seven weeks.

Owen was twenty-four years old. He was small, slightly built, strong, and known for his friendliness and generosity. His religious faith was his guiding force. He kept a diary of each day's activity, but at some point in his life, it was lost. Later he re-created it using a fellow traveler's journal to corroborate his memories.

Emigrants on the Oregon Trail that year numbered in the thousands. Large groups split into smaller units, sometimes rejoining and traveling near each other,

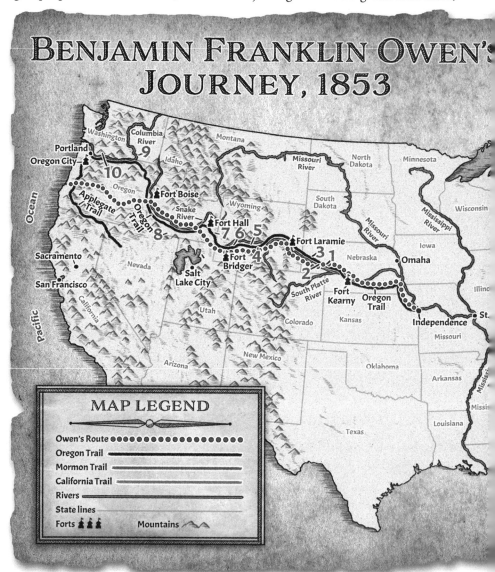

BENJAMIN FRANKLIN OWEN'S JOURNEY, 1853

MAP LEGEND

Owen's Route •••••••••••••••••••
Oregon Trail
Mormon Trail
California Trail
Rivers
State lines
Forts 🏛🏛🏛   Mountains ⌃⌃⌃

and other times widely spread out. In late July, after hundreds of miles on the trail, Owen and his companions overtook the McClure-Bond wagon train in present-day southern Idaho and felt a pleasant camaraderie with them, so joined their ranks.

It was a relatively uneventful trip until they reached a cutoff that veered from the main trail in today's eastern Oregon along the Malheur River. There, an optimistic and charismatic guide, Elijah Elliott, convinced some of them that the cutoff was a shorter route, with good grass and water for their trail-worn horses and oxen. The new way was less dusty, he said, and would bypass several treacherous areas on the established trail, enabling the emigrants to reach the settlements more quickly.

Elliott, however, had never traveled the cutoff himself, relying instead on what others had told him. The rough trail followed the route that pilot Stephen Meek had used in 1845; it had resulted in death and disaster when his party became disoriented in the eastern Oregon deserts and finally straggled into The Dalles with winter nipping at their heels.

The McClure-Bond wagon train, including Frank Owen and his two friends, decided to take the cutoff. Elijah Elliott and his party left the Oregon Trail in late August. Owen's train followed with nearly fifty wagons on September 1. More groups trailed behind, until the number of cutoff travelers totaled more than a thousand.

The emigrants made slow progress, realizing too late that the new route was

LANDMARK LEGEND

1. Courthouse Rock   6. South Pass
2. Chimney Rock   7. Soda Springs
3. Scotts Bluff   8. City of Rocks
4. Independence Rock   9. The Whitman Mission
5. Devil's Gate   10. The Dalles

perilous and particularly hard on the animals. Along with countless steep hills to traverse and bluffs to avoid, there was tough, shoulder-high sagebrush blocking the way and sharp stones underfoot that tore the oxen's hooves. After some time, the travelers had gone too far to return to the Oregon Trail, so they pressed on, moving farther and farther into the dry, uncharted country. Water and food supplies became scarce. Some people were sick, and the cattle were failing. It was obvious that Elliott, while still optimistic, didn't know what lay ahead. Possibly mistaking southeastern Oregon's massive Steen's Mountain for a southern branch of the Cascades, the travelers thought they were much farther west than they were.

On September 11, Owen and his friend Andrew S. McClure, twenty-four, from the McClure-Bond train, rode ahead to catch Elliott's party. By then, provisions were dangerously low. The cutoff trail was nearly impossible to follow, and winter was fast approaching. It was decided to send a relief party ahead to bring food from the settlements.

Eight young men from the spread-out wagon trains were selected for the job. Frank Owen, Andrew McClure, and the six others set out on horseback with seven days of limited rations on the morning of September 13. They expected to return with help in ten days or so.

Trouble began immediately when the relief party encountered undrinkable alkali water. Then they mired a prized horse in a stream. Pulling her out with ropes cost time and energy. Snow was creeping down the mountains as the men spent nearly five days skirting the enormous Malheur and Harney Lakes near today's town of Burns, Oregon. They sought the Deschutes River in the vicinity of present-day Bend, where the Free Emigrant Road would provide a primitive route through the Cascades to the Willamette Valley.

After nearly circumnavigating the two lakes, the men rode to the top of a high butte. There, only five or six miles away, they could see the spot where they had left Elliott's wagon train. Discouraged, and realizing that they had ridden in a giant circle, they conferred and turned northwest. Grass and drinkable water were scarce, and the horses were weak. The men had used up most of their rations on the fruitless endeavor. On September 19, Owen wrote in his journal that the day's drive was *"rather aimless, & unsatisfactory"* and they felt *"uncertain as to the headway we had made."*

Andrew McClure also kept a detailed diary, and he reported the next night that supper consisted of tea and a paste made of flour. But the following day, they were able to kill a sage hen and make soup. Though not enough nourishment for eight ravenous men, it raised their spirits.

The day after that, the travelers found water for themselves and the horses. Weak from hunger, they killed a small pack pony and spent the day eating their fill and drying meat for the hard miles ahead. Then they pushed on. Already, they were exhausted, and Owen's shoes were falling apart. When it rained, the men slurped water from hollows in the rocks. They revived when they caught sight of the lofty, snowcapped Three Sisters, which meant the Cascade Range was in view. But confusing one mountain with another, they spotted a pass between South Sister and Middle Sister that looked like the route they were seeking. Encouraged, they located and finally crossed the long-sought Deschutes River. It was September 25, nearly two weeks since they had started.

In the meantime, the wagon parties kept on, making slow, desperate progress. Illness, a terrible lack of water, and confusion about the route hampered them. Many anxious days had passed since Owen, McClure, and the others had left for the settlements, and the emigrants expected the men to return soon with help. Wisely, however, they continued to send scouts to search for the Deschutes and find aid. Their parched oxen and horses finally smelled the river and made a headlong rush for it, just a few days after the rescue party had passed there.

Owen and his companions, failing to spot the few blazed trees that signaled the Free Emigrant Road, headed immediately toward the pass between South Sister and Middle Sister and started up, only to discover deep ravines and dense evergreen forests. It was hard traveling with the horses, but they made slow progress. The men were sick with diarrhea and weak again from lack of food, but on September 28, Owen reported that they reached the summit. There a near-accident occurred, which Owen remembered all his life. The hammer of his gun, which was pointed in the direction of his friend McClure as they rode side by side, caught on a branch and was drawn back to the last notch. A fraction more and the gun would have fired. Both men reacted quickly, but Owen felt that McClure's death was averted because of the *"Kindly interposition of the Saviors hand."*

Travel was downhill then. At their next camping spot, the men found water, plenty of grass for the horses, and ripe huckleberries, which they "ate with a relish," according to McClure. They noted a hard frost that night. The western slopes of the Cascades were more impenetrable, lush, and wet than the eastern slopes. Huge Douglas-fir trees, fallen logs, and heavy undergrowth surrounded them. Deadfall impeded their progress. Locating a trail, they followed it for half a day, but it ended in thorny tangles of briers impassible for the horses. They had to backtrack, returning to the previous night's camp. Their pants were shredded around their legs, and the horses were sick.

The situation was grim. The men were famished, and the fallen timber was so thick it was nearly impossible to get through. Game eluded them. Grass was scarce in places, and the party traveled only a few miles each day. Still, they forged ahead and descended a ravine thousands of feet deep. Supper was *"hawk with soup,"* since their supply of pony meat had given out. The horses were failing fast. It was now October.

Somehow, they climbed out of the ravine. When one of the depleted animals fell and could not get up, they butchered it in a thicket. Camping nearby that night, the men ate their fill and jerked the rest of the meat to take with them.

The eight members of the relief party stayed together until October 3, when three of the men decided to leave their horses where there was grass and water and continue on foot. The other five, including Owen and McClure, wanted to keep their animals, their only certain source of food. Reluctantly, the company divided their meager supplies and split up. Owen noted that *"having undergone So many privations together It is No Wonder that at our Separation We all Wept like So many children."*

During the next few days, the Owen-McClure group made its way down the McKenzie River, fighting the harsh terrain. Hoping that the stream would take them to the settled valleys ahead, they followed it, despite the undergrowth. Much of the time, they splashed ahead in the cold river itself. Huckleberries and elderberries were their sustenance when the meat supply got low again. At one point, a dead salmon they found became dinner and breakfast.

Benjamin Franklin Owen followed the wild McKenzie River through the Cascade Range in his attempt to reach the Willamette Valley settlements and get help for his stranded wagon train. SHUTTERSTOCK. PHOTO BY MARISA ESTIVILL, ID: 512281846.

The river turned out to be nearly impassable. The discouraged men forded it time after time, but its bed was made of large stones, which were dangerous and difficult for the horses. The next day, one of the remaining animals was too weak to withstand the current and went tumbling downriver. It was butchered for food. A couple of days later (October 10), realizing that the remaining horses were worn out, the five men decided that they, too, had to leave their animals behind. They forged ahead on foot, taking only their blankets and guns. Two of the party wanted to travel faster, so they went on, leaving Owen, McClure, and their friend Robert Tandy behind. By then, the three were declining. Harsh, cold rain soaked them as fatigue and hunger slowed their pace. McClure confessed to feeling weak and dispirited. The terrain was still treacherous, and the meat was gone again, until Owen managed to kill two small squirrels and later, a pheasant. They struggled on, packing their heavy, wet blankets.

In the meantime, the wagon train travelers had finally located the Deschutes River and the Free Emigrant Road they had long pursued. They sent two new scouts, Ranson Kelly and young Martin Blanding, up the primitive road with a worn horse and some provisions. Then they continued their floundering progress into the Cascades. The narrow track was blocked with downed timber, boulders, creeks, and gullies, making it nearly impossible to get the wagons through. While Blanding and Kelly hurried toward the settlements, the men toiled day and night, often in the rain, to make the way barely passable.

Blanding and Kelly traveled for days with meager supplies. Finally, Kelly could not go on. Blanding had no choice but to leave him and continue alone. Close to starving he stumbled ahead, at last nearing the outermost settlements. He used his waning strength to build a campfire. The smoke caught the attention of some cattle herders nearby, and they found Blanding curled up by the flames. The men took him to a cabin, where he ate ravenously and told the story of his starving partner and the frantic wagon travelers behind him. Immediately, word went out to the surrounding villages and farms, and the settlers quickly put together dozens of pack animals and wagons loaded with provisions and supplies.

Meanwhile, Owen, McClure, and Tandy stumbled on. They were surprised when five teenagers came up from behind. The youths were additional scouts sent from the wagon trains and were traveling more quickly than the three, who by then had been journeying for a full month. The boys had killed enough game to last them to the valleys ahead. After a brief, unpleasant conversation about the possibility of using the boys' dog for food, they went on, apparently without sharing their provisions.

McClure's diary ended that day, October 13, 1853. Owen reported that his friend felt he could not travel any farther. McClure urged the other two to leave him, but they adamantly refused, heeding their code of friendship and decency. Together, the three moved slowly ahead.

Back on the Free Emigrant Road, the wagon parties were losing hope as the rough trail presented them with challenge after daunting challenge. Little did they know that the nearby villagers and farmers, heavily loaded with relief supplies, were hurrying to find them. When the settlers appeared bearing their lifesaving provisions, the depleted wagon travelers greeted them with tears of joy. After eating, resting, and profusely thanking their benefactors, the overlanders inched down the remaining western mountain slopes until they reached the outlying cabins and settlements. It took days for all the stragglers to get through. With winter looming, they needed shelter. Some spread out into the Willamette Valley and others spent the next few months with local families who took them in.

For Owen, McClure, and Tandy, still creeping toward civilization, the ordeal was not over. The weather was so wet that they used fibers from their clothing to start their evening fires. Once, they simply sat in the rain and ate a raw squirrel McClure had shot, saving the hide to roast in camp that night. For the next few days, they worked their way down the river, devouring whatever they could find, including another hawk, burned fish from an old campfire the teenagers had left, small squirrels, a bird they called a pheasant, and rose hips. Emaciated and exhausted, they made slow progress. Owen's shoes had disintegrated and he was barefoot.

Then, while picking and eating rose hips on October 20, they heard a man's voice call out. Six rescuers rode toward them, bearing *a nice lot of provisions,* Owen later jubilantly wrote. The leader, whom Owen called Uncle Isaac Briggs, had heard about their terrible plight from the teenage scouts and the three men who had initially left the rescue group. All had reached civilization in the vicinity of present-day Springfield, Oregon.

Immediately, the rescuers took over, giving Owen, McClure, and Tandy a light meal and restraining them from the eating too much until their starved bodies could manage more. They had brought shoes for Owen, and they helped their weakened companions travel to a campsite ahead. There, a blazing fire greeted them and they feasted on more nourishing food, including baked potatoes with melted butter, Owen reported with pleasure. After prayers of thanksgiving and a round of sacred songs, the men retired for the night.

From there, things happened quickly. Owen, McClure, and Tandy learned that the lost wagon train had already labored into the settlements, where their friends were being tended. Robert Tandy's family came out with a doctor and a horse so he could ride to safety. Owen and McClure finished their journey on foot and were welcomed into a series of settlers' homes for meals and care. Owen later wrote: *"It was just like coming into Paradice, or a land flowing with Milk, & Honey."*

Owen, and probably McClure, went on to the fledgling town of Eugene, where they met members of the wagon parties and returned the guns they had borrowed for the rescue attempt. Owen also found one of his friends from back home, and together they sold the old wagon they had used on the overland trail. Soon after, Owen, by then somewhat recovered, left for the gold mines in southern Oregon and California.

He later returned to Oregon, where he married Jane Curry McClure in 1859; they had fifteen children. Owen farmed and also learned and practiced homeopathic medicine. He often thought that he had fared better on the rescue mission than his companion McClure because of his own small, wiry physique. The scanty rations, he felt, had nourished his slight body more than his large friend McClure's.

Andrew McClure eventually settled in Eugene and is said to have run a dry goods store. At the age of thirty, he married Sarah Jane Dillard and they, too, had a large family. He later served briefly as Lane County Treasurer and was a member of the Odd Fellows. McClure and Owen remained friends all their lives.

The Lost Wagon Train of 1853 has gone down in history as one of the most difficult journeys on the overland trails. Although Benjamin Franklin Owen and his comrades were not successful in bringing aid, their story is notable for the loyalty, enduring friendship, and perseverance they showed during the dangerous ordeal to rescue their fellow travelers—and to save each other's lives.

DANGER ON THE
BLOODY BOZEMAN

The Story of Davis Willson

TWENTY-FOUR-YEAR-OLD Davis Willson slapped the mosquitoes biting his forearm, then squashed another on his neck. The wretched insects were everywhere, hovering in clouds and alighting on every living thing until even the tough-hided mules flinched from the constant aggravation. He'd never seen anything like them nor heard anything as irritating as their tiny piercing whine.

Good thing he'd brought along a mosquito net, which allowed him to sleep out here along the Platte River. Omaha, the small capitol of Nebraska Territory, seemed far away, although it had been only a few days since they'd departed from there on the Council Bluffs Road.

It was early June, 1866, and Willson had just traveled all the way to Omaha from Canton, New York, by rail and steamboat. He and eight New York friends and relatives had joined forces back

Davis Willson, pictured here with his nephew Fred. PHOTO-GRAPH COURTESY OF MONTANA STATE UNIVERSITY LIBRARY, MERRILL G. BURLINGAME SPECIAL COLLECTIONS, PETER KOCH NELSON PAPERS, 1944-1957.

east, where his older brother, Lester, had helped mastermind this journey. Lester had stayed behind in New York, but promised to join his brother in Montana the following year.

Once in Omaha, the nine emigrants had acquired wagons and loaded them with goods, intent on establishing a mercantile in the fledgling town of Bozeman, Montana Territory.

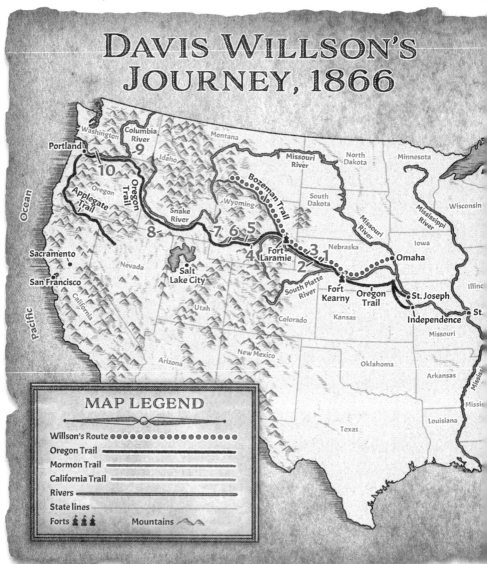

Being on the trail was a far cry from the life Willson had known for the past several years. In his youth, his health had been poor, so he'd spent months in California, hoping the warm climate would help. Then he'd returned home to New York and attended three years of college, working for newspapers to help support himself. His fourth and final year was at Oberlin College in Ohio. As the Civil War dragged on, he served a stint with the Union Army. But despite this diverse background, coaxing mules across a muddy, mosquito-infested trail to the West was a new adventure for him.

The company called itself the Tuller and Rich overland party, named for business partners and travel companions Loren Tuller and Charlie Rich. The remaining seven men had been hired to help transport the merchandise in three covered wagons to Bozeman.

Willson kept a journal of the trip and also wrote letters to his family, especially Lester. Literate and careful with his wording, his pleasant personality shines through in his diary, which is filled with humor, reflection, and optimism. Willson also described the group's daily activities, the beautiful landscapes they passed, and the people they met. During the journey's first week, he reported that they had encountered a traveler he nicknamed "Blowhard," whom he described as a *greasy man* with black teeth, a braggart who was transporting a load of whiskey to Montana Territory. Later in the trip, he would retract his words.

Willson brought along his violin and played it often, his music brightening many

LANDMARK LEGEND

1. Courthouse Rock	6. South Pass
2. Chimney Rock	7. Soda Springs
3. Scotts Bluff	8. City of Rocks
4. Independence Rock	9. The Whitman Mission
5. Devil's Gate	10. The Dalles

a dull moment or dreary evening. His positivity was evident. Even his description of a long, cold night on guard duty ("about the longest night that ever darkened the country") was balanced with four cheerful words: *"But morning always comes."*

By 1866, the Council Bluffs Road along the north bank of the Platte was well established, with basic amenities that earlier travelers didn't enjoy. Farmhouses, simple hotels, and small stores dotted the landscape. During the mid-1860s, the route was heavily traveled. The many wagon parties would allow other groups to pass them and then they would catch up again. Some companies encountered each other again and again.

But the end of overland wagon travel was in sight: For the first couple of weeks, Willson's company journeyed near the new Union Pacific railroad tracks. Trains were replacing covered wagons as a primary means of travel to the West.

One night early in the trip, Willson reported a frightening thunderstorm with high winds. The next morning, he noted, he made breakfast wrapped in his mosquito net. His companions, who had earlier poked fun at his net, had since spent such miserable nights that they changed their tune. Someone even offered to buy it from him for three dollars. Willson declined.

Little did the Tuller and Rich party know that trouble was brewing ahead. Their plan was to turn off onto the 500-mile-long Bozeman Trail (named for early promoter John Bozeman), which stretched from the North Platte River near present-day Casper, Wyoming, through Dakota and Montana Territories. The trail wound across prime hunting lands of the Lakota Sioux, Northern Cheyenne, and Arapaho peoples along an ancient travel corridor. After gold was discovered at Montana's Grasshopper Creek in 1862, the route was used by white gold seekers without consent. During 1864 and 1865, several thousand emigrants made the trip. Conflict between the influx of settlers and the indigenous peoples broke out.

In 1865 and 1866, United States troops built three forts along the Bozeman Trail—Fort Reno, Fort Phil Kearny, and Fort C. F. Smith—to protect wagon travelers bound for the Montana goldfields. Enraged by this military presence and further invasion of their lands, native warriors fought back. In 1866, just as Willson's

Chief Red Cloud of the Oglala Lakota Sioux, shown here in 1872, was instrumental in organizing resistance to early emigrant invasions into his people's lands. PHOTOGRAPH COURTESY OF HISTORY NEBRASKA PHOTOGRAPH COLLECTIONS, RG2063-101116.

company was winding its way up the Platte, indigenous and U.S. government leaders assembled at Fort Laramie to discuss the issue. Oglala Lakota Sioux Chief Red Cloud could see the handwriting on the wall: The U.S. government was going to keep the road open with or without his people's consent. This triggered a two-year war, now known as Red Cloud's War, characterized by continuous raids on emigrant trains and the forts.

Willson and his companions were heading straight into the conflict.

With little idea what was in store for them, the men went about their business, stopping for the Sabbath and swimming in the turbid Platte. Willson was upset when one of his close companions got intoxicated at Fort Kearny and nearly drowned swimming across the river back to camp. To Willson, such behavior put a strain on their relationship.

Near the end of June, eighteen or twenty mounted men, possibly Sioux, appeared, requesting food. They advised Willson and his friends not to sleep when they got past Fort Laramie, indicating that there was danger beyond that point. Later, when the wagon party encountered the same riders again, they were in war paint. Willson and his friends were wary and fearful, not knowing what to expect, but nothing came of the incident.

The road got rougher as the Tuller and Rich party moved into today's southeast Wyoming and passed through at least one native village. They stopped across the North Platte from Fort Laramie before crossing over by ferry. There they would join the first mule train that happened along, increasing their numbers for safety. Later Willson noted that they had merged with a train of freight wagons called the Phillips and Freeland Company, *"a hard set."* Shortly after leaving Fort Laramie, this larger group crossed the North Platte again.

Willson celebrated his twenty-fifth birthday on July 17. Even though he was exhausted from the hard travel, he wrote a letter to Lester and played his violin. A couple of days later, the party of twenty-four wagons veered onto the cutoff that led to the Bozeman Trail, where the men became fully aware of their dangerous situation.

On Sunday, July 22, the group had stopped for lunch when a small war party tried to stampede their animals. Well-armed, the travelers managed to rebuff the attempt. But Willson's train was more cautious after that, posting guards on all sides as they hurried toward Antelope Creek, the night's campsite.

At dawn the next morning, warriors again attempted to raid the stock. Again, they were driven off with gunfire. A third attempt took place on July 24 as the travelers were watering their animals. After firing shots until the warriors withdrew, the emigrants started up again and drove without stopping until dark, camping on the Dry Fork of the Powder River.

On July 26, the tense party gratefully reached the remote Fort Reno in today's northeastern Wyoming. There they heard stories about more violent altercations. Camping near the newly built log stockade, the men waited for several days until more wagons arrived to fortify their numbers. Willson detailed the deaths that had resulted from skirmishes with other wagon parties. One train had lost eight people; another had lost two. Warriors had been killed as well. The man Willson had earlier called "Blowhard" was dead and mutilated. Willson noted that he regretted naming him as he had in his journal, hinting that the man had not deserved his brutal death.

By the end of the month, Willson reported that about 200 wagons had assembled with nearly 300 men. They felt it was safe to go on. But rain swelled the Powder River and delayed the journey again. Finally, on August 1, the huge wagon train pulled out with what Willson called *"dark forebodings."* Armed and watchful, they wound their way toward Fort Phil Kearny, which was about fifty miles ahead in today's northcentral Wyoming.

Even under stress, Willson mentioned again and again the striking beauty of the vast, untouched landscape. Journal entries describe the scenic Bighorn Mountains and broad, pleasant valleys. But his writings also indicated the party's uneasiness. He reported one day that their herders fired at a rabbit, and the whole jittery company, thinking they were under attack, grabbed their firearms for a fight.

They traveled relentlessly, trying to get through the dangerous area as quickly as possible, but the sheer number of lumbering wagons along with two droves of cattle made travel sluggish. By August 5, the group arrived at Fort Phil Kearny. They were told to camp far from the stockade to preserve feed for the government animals. Willson took inventory of the wagon train, itemizing firearms and ammunition, men, and animals for the fort's commander. He also wrote again to Lester and mailed his letter there.

As they pulled away from the stockade, they had to wait for the wagons ahead to ford a difficult stream and struggle up some steep hills. While they paused, the fort's band, which may have included as many as forty brass instruments, began to play. As the music drifted his way, Willson was moved by a wave of emotion. He wrote a long diary entry that day, putting down his sentiments about the wild beauty surrounding him and his fond thoughts of home before the wagons pushed on.

At the top of a high ridge, the view of the surrounding landscape was spectacular, but descending was difficult. The wagons had to slide down one at a time with their wheels locked. That twelve-hour day, they covered only about five miles.

Scouts rode ahead to watch for danger as the long, dusty train progressed. The men enjoyed borrowing a field glass from the company's guide, examining their surroundings with it. Willson took part, but made a point of staying with the wagons and carrying his gun. A group of Arapaho appeared on a bluff, raising a flag of truce. The guide met them and offered them tobacco, which they took before moving on.

Willson reported seeing antelope, buffalo, and signs of grizzlies. Wolves howled at night, and fish swam in the clear streams. He noticed birds he called sage hens and buffalo birds. At one point, a small herd of bison was startled by his presence and started to run. Willson enjoyed watching them thunder away, *"snorting at every step. . . ."*

He also began noting which of the assembled wagon parties was in the lead. Overland travelers often tried to outpace each other to reach important points on the trails. Sometimes it was done in friendly rivalry, but it could turn acrimonious and highly competitive. At first, Willson called it *"A good deal of sport."* By mid-August, though, the cutthroat competition had turned hostile.

Their route brought them to the third and last new garrison, Fort C. F. Smith, near the Bighorn River in Montana Territory. Soldiers posted at this remote location were under such constant threat of danger that a substantial number of them deserted. Some suffered mental struggles, almost certainly from fear and isolation. Willson was among the first travelers to reach the fort and mentioned the aggression among wagon parties vying to cross the Bighorn River. Shouting, arguing, and the sound of cracking whips filled the air while drivers tried to cut each other off. A ferry was available at a cost of five dollars per wagon.

The road got rougher, with steep ravines and what Willson called a volcanic badlands. The mules were worn out, but were still being driven hard. Everyone was weary and irritable. The August day they arrived at a viewpoint over the beautiful Rosebud Valley, they awakened before 3:00 A.M. to get ahead of the other trains. They had to double-lock the wagon brakes as they descended to the stony road below, where they had the backbreaking work of picking rocks. Willson was tired, but also encouraged because they were getting near the Yellowstone River, which they would follow almost to Bozeman. He mentioned having a bad headache and feeling anxious seeing recently dug graves of emigrants killed by war parties. His feet hurt so much at one point that he walked with one boot on and one boot off.

The tone of his diary brightened as the end of the journey drew near. His violin provided a welcome diversion to the exhausted group. There were difficult roads and heavy rain, but he wrote that his friends caught fine messes of fish, which they undoubtedly cooked over their evening campfires and savored with pleasure. He made note of a beautiful spot where he dreamed of establishing a ranch or a home. Some of the men enjoyed picking ripe gooseberries, and they paused to rest at a refreshing little spring that bubbled from the ground.

A simple fence told them they were approaching the small settlement of Bozeman. The men cheered in jubilation when they saw it, then cheered again as they passed cultivated fields and a couple of ranches. Willson felt a weight lift from his tired shoulders. After the tense journey up the Bozeman Trail, they had arrived safely in "Bozeman City." According to Willson, the town had about six buildings. It was September 2, 1866.

Almost immediately, the nine Tuller and Rich friends split up. Some found work in Bozeman while others went on to Helena. Although most of them returned to Bozeman, Willson lamented the separation. He had grown up with these men and travelled for weeks under dangerous conditions with them. From the sadness expressed in his diary, his companions were like brothers to him.

Lester, true to his word, joined Willson in Bozeman the following year. Loren Tuller and Charlie Rich set up their mercantile in a tent and later moved it into a small building. Lester entered into a partnership with them and eventually took over the operation, beginning a long, profitable retail career.

Davis Willson and his brother Lester, in partnership with others, opened the Tuller and Rich Cheap Cash Store in 1866. It is shown here in what may be the oldest known photograph of Bozeman, Montana. PHOTOGRAPH COURTESY OF MONTANA STATE UNIVERSITY LIBRARY, MERRILL G. BURLINGAME SPECIAL COLLECTIONS, LESTER S. WILLSON FAMILY PAPERS, 1861-1922.

By 1867, Davis Willson was teaching school and working at the mercantile. He later took various bookkeeping and clerical jobs. In 1872, he became a founding member of Bozeman's First Presbyterian Church. He reportedly returned to the East for his father's funeral in the early 1870s, and that was where he met and courted Martha Van Allen. The young woman later traveled more than 2,000 miles to join her promised husband in Bozeman. They were married in 1874.

Willson was elected a church trustee in 1879, when the decision was made to construct a First Presbyterian church building. He served as an elder there for several years. In October 1889, fulfilling a long-held dream, he was ordained to the ministry and went on to serve two Presbyterian congregations in nearby Hamilton (modern-day Manhattan) and Springhill. His congregants, to whom he ministered for more than twenty years, knew him to be congenial and gentle.

He and Martha, also an active member of the church, had one son, Frank Gardner Willson, who grew up in the Bozeman area. The couple remained there for the rest of their lives.

The Bozeman Trail was short-lived. Two years after Davis Willson made his journey, after continual resistance by Red Cloud and his allies, the Fort Laramie Treaty of 1868 was created. Intended to put a stop to the deadly disputes along the Bozeman Trail, it set forth the boundaries of the Great Sioux Reservation, which included all of today's state of South Dakota west of the Missouri River. It recognized the Black Hills (a region sacred to the Sioux) as an integral part of the territory, reserved for the Sioux people's exclusive use. Conditions of the treaty included abandonment of the three forts. The Bozeman Trail was closed and the forts were burned. Red Cloud had been victorious.

In the 1870s, however, when gold was discovered in the Black Hills, the United States government rewrote the parameters of the treaty and confiscated the sacred area; today this remains at the center of a land dispute between the Sioux Nation and the U.S. government.

Davis Willson's coming-of-age story centers on the Bozeman Trail, known to historians as the Bloody Bozeman. Passing safely over the trail in the tense year of 1866 undoubtedly had a significant effect on the rest of his life. Grateful to have reached his destination, he settled in Bozeman with purpose. Then, he went on to live the life he envisioned in the beautiful Montana setting that became his new home.

BIBLIOGRAPHY

For William T. Newby:

Applegate, Jesse. "A Day with the Cow Column in 1843." *The Quarterly of the Oregon Historical Society,* vol. 1, no. 4 (Dec. 1900): 371–83. JSTOR. http://www.jstor.org/stable/20609477.

Edwards, G. Thomas. "Marcus Whitman, 1802-1847." *Oregon Encyclopedia: A Project of the Oregon Historical Society.* Last updated Mar. 29, 2022. https://www.oregonencyclopedia.org/articles/whitman_marcus/#.YpqO4-xMEwD

Flora, Stephanie. "The Emigration to Oregon Country in 1843." *oregonpioneers.com.* 2017. http://www.oregonpioneers.com/1843trip.htm

Galvez, Gilberto. "Philanthropists Save Linfield, Donate Names." *The Linfield Review,* May 7, 2014. https://thelinfieldreview.com/16194/features/philanthropists-save-linfield-donate-names/

Linscheid, Dan. "McMinnville." *Oregon Encyclopedia: A Project of the Oregon Historical Society.* Last updated June 14, 2022. https://www.oregonencyclopedia.org/articles/mcminnville/#.YmxuctrMJ9A

National Park Service: Fort Vancouver. "Dr. John McLoughlin, Chief Factor of Fort Vancouver." Last updated May 27, 2016. https://www.nps.gov/fova/drjohnmcloughlin.htm

Nesmith, James W. "Diary of the Emigration of 1843." *The Quarterly of the Oregon Historical Society,* vol. 7, no. 4 (1906): 329–59. JSTOR. https://www.jstor.org/stable/20609704

"Newby, Sarah Jane (McGary) 1823-1887." *Oregon Historical Society Digital Collections.* 2017. https://digitalcollections.ohs.org/newby-sarah-jane-mcgary

"Newby, William T. 1820-1884." *Oregon Historical Society Digital Collections.* 2017. https://digitalcollections.ohs.org/newby-william-t?listPage=2&sort=identifier&listLimit=28

Van Heukelem, Christy, Tom Fuller, and the News-Register. *McMinnville (Images of America).* Charleston, S.C.: Arcadia Publishing, 2012.

Winton, Harry N. M. "William T. Newby's Diary of the Emigration of 1843."
    Oregon Historical Quarterly vol. 40, no. 3 (1939): 219–42. JSTOR.
    http://www.jstor.org/stable/20611196.

For Patrick Breen:

Breen, Patrick. "Patrick Breen Diary." *Online Archive of California.*
    Contributor: University of California, The Bancroft Library, 2011.
    https://oac.cdlib.org/ark:/28722/bk0004b217j/?brand=oac4

Brown, Daniel James. *The Indifferent Stars Above; The Harrowing Saga of the Donner Party.*
    New York: William Morrow, 2009.

Burns, Ric. *The American Experience: The Donner Party, A Film by Ric Burns.*
    PBS: Distributed by Warner Home Video. 2003.

Enright, John Shea., S.J., "The Breens of San Juan Bautista: With a Calendar of Family
    Papers." *California Historical Society Quarterly,* vol. 33, no. 4, 349–59, 1954.
    University of California Press. https://doi.org/10.2307/25156521

Johnson, Kristin, ed. "Virginia Reed Murphy (1833–1921)." In *Unfortunate Emigrants.*
    University Press of Colorado, 1996: 262–86. https://doi.org/10.2307/j.ctt46nr9n.17

McGlashan, Charles F. *History of the Donner Party: A Tragedy of the Sierra.*
    Barnes & Noble Publishing, Inc., 2004.

National Park Service. "Jose Castro House, San Juan Bautista, California." n.d.
    https://www.nps.gov/nr/travel/american_latino_heritage/Jose_Castro_House.html

Rarick, Ethan. *Desperate Passage: The Donner Party's Perilous Journey West.*
    New York: Oxford University Press, Inc., 2008.

Stuart, George R., ed. *The Diary of Patrick Breen: Recounting the Ordeal of the Donner
    Party Snowbound in the Sierra 1846-47.* San Francisco: L.D. Allen Press, 1946.

Stewart, George R. *Ordeal by Hunger: The Story of the Donner Party.*
    Boston & New York, Houghton Mifflin, 1988.

Stuckey, Mary E. "The Donner Party and the Rhetoric of Westward Expansion."
    Rhetoric and Public Affairs vol. 14, no. 2 (2011): 229–60. JSTOR.
    http://www.jstor.org/stable/41940539.

For William Swain:

Holliday, J. S. "In the Diggings." *California History,* vol. 61, no. 3 (1982): 168–87.
    University of California Press. https://doi.org/10.2307/25158109

Holliday, J. S. "Reverberations of the California Gold Rush." *California History,* vol. 77, no. 1 (1998): 4–15. *University of California Press.* https://doi.org/10.2307/25462458

Holliday, J. S. and William Swain. *The World Rushed in: The California Gold Rush Experience.* New York: Simon and Schuster, 1981.

Rawls, James J. "Great Expectations: William Swain, J.S. Holliday & the World Rushed In." *California History,* vol. 61, no. 3. (1982): 162–67. *University of California Press.* https://doi.org/10.2307/25158108

Smith, Diana. "Guide to the J. S. Holliday Research Collection on the William Swain Family." *Yale of Western Americana, Beinecke Rare Book and Manuscript Library.* July 2001. https://archives.yale.edu/repositories/11/resources/1268

Swain, Sara Sabrina. "Swain Homestead." *New York History,* vol. 18, no. 1 (1937): 46–49. JSTOR. http://www.jstor.org/stable/23134563

Swain, William. "William Swain Letter Written from 'The Diggings' in California." *PBS: Ken Burns Presents The West: A Film by Stephen Ives.* 2023. https://www.pbs.org/kenburns/the-west/letter-from-william-swain-to-george-swain-1850

For James Wilkins:

Morgan, Dale L. *The Western Historical Quarterly,* vol.1, no. 1 (1970): 77–79. *Oxford Academic.* https://doi.org/10.2307/967406

Murphy, David Royce. "The Art of the Panorama," *Nebraska History* vol. 92, 2011: 40-41.

Palmquist, Peter E. and Thomas R. Kailbourn. *Pioneer Photographers from the Mississippi to the Continental Divide: A Biographical Dictionary, 1839-1865.* Stanford University Press, 2005: 634-635.

Wilkins, James F. (John Francis McDermott, ed.). *An Artist on the Overland Trail.* The Huntington Library, San Marino, California, 1968.

"An Artist on the Overland Trail—Image Gallery Essay: The 1849 Sketches of James F. Wilkins." *Wisconsin Historical Society.* 1996-2023. https://www.wisconsinhistory.org/Records/Article/CS3757

"James F. Wilkins: Categories of Western Historical Images." *Wisconsin Historical Society.* 1996-2023. https://www.wisonsinhistory.org/Records? &terms=James%2cF.%2cWilkins&facets=CATEGORIES%3a%22Wisconsin+ Images%22

BIBLIOGRAPHY

For Alvin Aaron Coffey:

Clark, Robert, with Don Buck, Tom Hunt, and Will Bagley, "The Autobiography of Alvin A Coffey." *Overland Journal: Quarterly of the Oregon-California Trails Association,* vol. 20, no. 2, Summer 2002: 64-73.

Coffey, Alvin Aaron. "Autobiography and Reminiscence of Alvin Aaron Coffey," Mills Seminary P.O., 1901. *Online Archive of California.* Contributor: The Society of California Pioneers, Alice Phelan Sullivan Library, San Francisco. https://oac.cdlib.org/ark:/13030/kt0c6018fg/?order=2&brand=oac4

"Coffey, Alvin A.," *Notable Kentucky African Americans Database.* Last modified Sept. 14, 2017. https://nkaa.uky.edu/nkaa/items/show/859

Hale, Israel F. "Diary of a Trip to California in 1849." *Merrill J. Mattes Collection: The Oregon-California Trails Association,* 2016. https://www.octa-journals.org/merrill-mattes-collection/diary-of-trip-to-california-israel-f-hale-1849

Lapp, Rudolph M. *Blacks in Gold Rush California.* New Haven and London: Yale University Press, 1977.

"Alvin A. Coffey." *LocalWiki* (Oakland). 2022. https://localwiki.org/oakland/Alvin_A._Coffey

Molson, Jeannette L. "Alvin Aaron Coffey (1822-1902)." *BlackPast.org.* May 19, 2020. https://blackpast.org/african-american-history/coffey-alvin-aaron-1822-1902/

Molson, Jeannette L., and Eual D. Blansett, Jr. *The Torturous Road to Freedom: The Life of Alvin Aaron Coffey.* Coppell, Texas: CreateSpace Independent Publishing Platform, 2014.

Moore, Shirley Ann Wilson. *Sweet Freedom's Plains: African Americans on the Overland Trails, 1841-1869.* Norman: University of Oklahoma Press, 2016.

For William Lewis Manley:

"Asabel and Sarah Bennett." *The Oregon-California Trails Association.* 2018. https://octa-trails.org/emigrant-profiles/asabel-sarah-bennett/

"Rancho San Francisco Historical Landmark." *California Office of Historic Preservation.* 2023. https://ohp.parks.ca.gov/listedresources/Detail/556

Manly, William Lewis. *Death Valley in '49: An Important Chapter of California Pioneer History.* New York and Santa Barbara: Wallace Hebberd, 1929.

Manly, William Lewis. *Death Valley in '49: The Autobiography of a Pioneer.* Santa Barbara: The Narrative Press, 2001.

Manly, W. L. "William Lewis Manly's Map." *Santa Clarita Valley Historical Society.* n.d. https://scvhistory.com/scvhistory/hs9401.htm

McCormic, David. "Naming of the New Park at Jayhawkers Place and William Manly St." *City of San Jose.* May 18, 2017. https://www.sanjoseca.gov/Home/ShowDocument?id=48167

Meyer, Mary Murdoch. "Timpanogos Nation." 2015. http://www.timpanogostribe.com/

National Park Service. "Death Valley National Park: The Lost '49ers." Last updated Oct. 1, 2021. https://www.nps.gov/deva/learn/historyculture/the-lost-49ers.htm

Novo, Marla. "Artifact of the Month: The Arcan Family Tablecloth." *Santa Cruz Museum of Art & History.* Aug 1, 2018. https://www.santacruzmah.org/blog/arcan-family-tablecloth

Wheat, Carl I. "The Forty-Niners in Death Valley: A Tentative Census." *Historical Society of Southern California Quarterly,* Dec. 1939. *Santa Clarita Valley Historical Society.* https://scvhistory.com/scvhistory/wheat-49ers.htm

For William Henry Hart:

Hart, William Henry. "Hart, William Henry vol 1. 1829-1888." *Digital Collections, BYU Library.* https://contentdm.lib.byu.edu/digital/collection/Diaries/id/7140/rec/1

Hart, William Henry. "Hart, William Henry vol 2. 1829-1888." *Digital Collections, BYU* Library. https://contentdm.lib.byu.edu/digital/collection/Diaries/id/7649/rec/26

"Placerville, California." *Western Mining History.* 2020. https://westernmininghistory.com/towns/california/placerville/

Schroath, Garrett. "William Henry Hart Diaries, Scope and Contents." *BYU Library Special Collections.* Mar. 2011. http://archives.lib.byu.edu/repositories/14/resources/5551

Stimson, Joni Poppitz. "Hart, William Henry, 1829-1888." *Utah Academic Library Consortium,* 2002. https://contentdm.lib.byu.edu/digital/collection/Biographies/id/18/rec/1

"The California Gold Rush." *Western Mining History.* 2020. https://westernmininghistory.com/5668/the-california-gold-rush/

For John Hudson Wayman:

Carter, Robert W. "Sometimes When I Hear the Winds Sigh: Mortality on the Overland Trail." *California History* vol. 74, no. 2 (1995): 146–61. *University of California Press.* https://doi.org/10.2307/25177489

"John Hudson Wayman: 15 July 1819—15 January 1867."
FamilySearch: The Church of Jesus Christ of Latter-day Saints. 2021.
https://ancestors.familysearch.org/en/KCKD-HLZ/john-hudson-wayman-1819-1867

Nemec, Bethany. "Doctors and Diseases on the Oregon Trail."
End of the Oregon Trail: Historic Oregon City. April 2, 2019.
https://historicoregoncity.org/2019/04/02/doctors-and-diseases-on-the-oregon-trail/

Olch, Peter D. "Treading The Elephant's Tail: Medical Problems on the Overland Trails."
Bulletin of the History of Medicine vol. 59, no. 2 (1985): 196–212. JSTOR.
https://www.jstor.org/stable/44441831

Pedersen, Elaine L. "Deciphering the Ormsby Gown: What Does It Tell?"
Nevada Historical Society Quarterly vol. 38, no. 2 (Summer 1995): 75-88.
http://epubs.nsla.nv.gov/statepubs/epubs/210777-1995-2Summer.pdf

Read, Georgia Willis. "Diseases, Drugs, and Doctors on the Oregon-California Trail in
the Gold-Rush Years." *Missouri Historical Review* vol. 38, no. 3, April 1944: 260-276.

Wayman, John Hudson. *A Doctor on the California Trail: The Diary of Dr. John Hudson
Wayman From Cambridge City, Indiana, to the Gold Fields in 1852.* Denver:
Old West Publishing Company, 1971.

For Benjamin Franklin Owen:

Beckham, Stephen Dow. *The Oregon Central Military Wagon Road: A History
and Reconnaissance.* Eugene, Oregon: U.S. Forest Service. 1981.
http://npshistory.com/publications/usfs/region/6/willamette/hrar-6.pdf

McNary, Lawrence A. "Route of Meek Cut-off, 1845." *Oregon Historical Quarterly*
vol. 35, no. 1 (1934): 1-9. JSTOR. www.jstor.org/stable/20610846

Menefee, Leah Collins, and Lowell Tiller. "Cutoff Fever, III." *Oregon Historical Quarterly*
vol. 78, no. 2 (1977): 121-57. JSTOR. www.jstor.org/stable/20613567

Menefee, Leah Collins, and Lowell Tiller. "Cutoff Fever, IV." *Oregon Historical Quarterly*
vol. 78, no. 3 (1977): 207-50. JSTOR. https://www.jstor.org/stable/20613576

Menefee, Leah Collins, and Lowell Tiller. "Cutoff Fever, V." *Oregon Historical Quarterly*
vol. 78, no. 4 (1977): 293-331. JSTOR. www.jstor.org/stable/20613590

McClure, Andrew S. "Andrew S. McClure Journal, 1853." *University of Oregon
Special Collections Manuscripts and Rare Books."* Sept. 2022.
https://oregondigital.org/concern/generics/df737p454?locale=en

"The Free Emigrant Road: An Oregon Historic Trail." *U.S. Forest Service.* n.d.
https://www.fs.usda.gov/Internet/FSE_DOCUMENTS/stelprd3843801.pdf

Owen, Benjamin Franklin. "My Trip Across the Plains: March 31, 1853—
October 28, 1853." *oregonpioneers.com*. n.d. http://www.oregonpioneers.com/
BFOwenDiary.pdf

Owen, Daniel. *The Lost Rescue: The Story of the Lost Wagon Train and the Men Who Tried to Save It*. CreateSpace Independent Publishing Platform: printed by the author, 2015.

For Davis Willson:

Badget, Mark and Mary Ellen McWilliams. "Along the Bozeman Trail." *Fort Phil Kearny Historic Site: National Historic Landmark and Interpretive Center*. 1985.
https://www.fortphilkearny.com/bozemantrail

Cutlip, Kimbra. "In 1868, Two Nations Made a Treaty, the U.S. Broke It and Plains Indian Tribes are Still Seeking Justice." *Smithsonian Magazine*, Nov. 2017.
https://www.smithsonianmag.com/smithsonian-institution/1868-two-nations-made-
treaty-us-broke-it-and-plains-indian-tribes-are-still-seeking-justice-180970741/

Doyle, Susan Badger, ed. *Bound for Montana: Diaries from the Bozeman Trail*.
Helena: The Montana Historical Society Press, 2004, 151-202.

Doyle, Susan Badger, ed. *Journeys to the Land of Gold: Emigrant Diaries from the Bozeman Trail, 1863-1866*, vols. 1 & 2. Helena: Montana Historical Society Press, 2000.

Drew, Marilyn J. "A Brief History of the Bozeman Trail." *WyoHistory.org: A Project of the Wyoming Historical Society*, Nov. 20, 2014.
https://www.wyohistory.org/encyclopedia/brief-history-bozeman-trail

McDermott, John D. *Red Cloud: Oglala Legend*. Pierre: South Dakota Historical Society Press, 2015.

Edwards, George, ed. *The Pioneer Work of the Presbyterian Church in Montana*.
Helena: Independent Publishing Company, n.d. https://static1.squarespace.com/
static/590be125ff7c502a07752a5b/t/5c6b22eaeb39312979e49e28/155052517967
1Edwards%2C+George%2C+The+Pioneer+Work+of+the+Presbyterian+Church+
in+Montana.pdf

"Our Story." *The Willson Company*, 2018
https://www.thewillsoncompany.com/our-story/

Ostlind, Emilene. "Red Cloud's War." *WyoHistory.org: A Project of the Wyoming Historical Society*, Nov. 8, 2014. https://www.wyohistory.org/encyclopedia/red-clouds-war

Scott, Kim Allen, "The Willson Brothers Come to Montana," *Montana: The Magazine of Western History*, vol. 49, no. 1 (Spring 1999): 58-71.

BIBLIOGRAPHY

"Treaty of Fort Laramie (1868)." *U.S. National Archives and Records Administration.* Last reviewed Mar. 29, 2022. https://www.archives.gov/milestone-documents/ fort-laramie-treaty#:~:text=In%20this%20treaty%2C%20signed%20on,use%20 by%20the%20Sioux%20people

Willson, Davis. "Collection 1076: Davis Willson Papers, 1861-1915." *Montana State University Library: Archives and Special Collections.* Last updated Mar. 5, 2009. https://www.lib.montana.edu/archives/finding-aids/1076.html

General Sources:

Faragher, John Mack. *Women and Men on the Overland Trail.* New Haven: Yale University Press, 1979.

Ives, Stephen, Jody Abramson, Geoffrey C. Wood, Dayton Duncan, and Ken Burns. *The West.* Alexandria, Virginia: PBS Video, 1996.

McLynn, Frank. *Wagons West: The Epic Story of America's Overland Trails.* New York: Grove Press, 2002.

"Trails West: Marking the Emigrant Trails to California." *Trails West, Inc.* 2010. https://emigranttrailswest.org/virtual-tour/california-trail/

Ward, Geoffrey C. *The West: An Illustrated History.* Boston, New York, Toronto, and London: Little, Brown, and Company, 1996.

Maps:

Jim Gatchell Museum Association, Inc. "The Bozeman Trail." Buffalo, Wyoming, 2000. *Fort Phil Kearny Historic Site: National Historic Landmark and Interpretive Center.* https://www.fortphilkearny.com/bozeman-trail-map

National Park Service. "California National Historic Trail Topographical Map." 2021. Last updated Aug. 31, 2021. https://www.nps.gov/cali/planyourvisit/upload/ National_Park_Service_California_Trail_Map-508.pdf

National Park Service. "Old Spanish National Historic Trail." 2021. Last updated Oct. 4, 2021. https://www.nps.gov/olsp/planyourvisit/maps.htm

National Park Service. "Oregon National Historic Trail Topographical Map." 2021. Last updated Aug. 31, 2021. https://www.nps.gov/oreg/planyourvisit/upload/ National-Park-Service-Oregon-Trail-Map-508.pdf

INDEX

Page numbers in **bold** indicate images.

Death Valley in '49 (Manly), 60
Deschutes River, 96, 97, 100
Devil's Gate, **x–xi**, 13, 31, 42, **43**, 77, 88
Dillard, Sarah Jane, 102
doctors. *See* physicians
Dolan, Patrick, 11, 16, 20
Donner, Elizabeth, 11
Donner, George, 10–11, 14, 20
Donner, Jacob, 11
Donner, Tamsen, 11
Donner Lake, 15, **16**
Donner Party, 10–23, 33
Dry Fork, 108
dysentery, 28–29

E
Echo Canyon, **78**
Elliott, Elijah, 95–96
Emery, Mrs., 76
emigration, ix–xiv
enslaved persons. *See* Coffey, Alvin Aaron
Eugene, OR, 102

F
Feather River, 34, 35
First Presbyterian Church, 112
Forest City, CA, 91
Forlorn Hope expedition, 19, 20
Fort Boise, 6
Fort Bridger, 5, 13, 44–45, **44**, 78
Fort C. F. Smith, 106, 110
Fort Hall, 6, 90
Fort Kearny, 29, 87, 93
Fort Laramie, 4, 13, 29, 30–31, 41, 53, 60, 76, 88, 107–108

Fort Laramie Treaty (1868), 112
Fort Phil Kearny, 106, 109
Fort Reno, 106, 108
Fort Vancouver, 7, 8
Fort Walla Walla, 7
Forty Mile Desert, 14–15, 46, 54, 79, 90
Fourth of July celebrations, 4, 13, 30–31, 42, 77, 89
Franciscan missions, 11
Free Emigrant Road, 96, 97, 100
freight wagons, x
Fremont, CA, 56

G
Genoa, NV, 91
Georgetown, CA, 71
goldfields: California, 24, 27, 35–36, 38, 59, 80–83, **80–81**; Montana, 106; Nevada, 91–92; South Dakota, 112
Goose Lake, 33, 55
Graham, George, 82
Grasshopper Creek, 106
Great Basin Desert, 64, 79
Great Divide, 44
Great Lakes, 25
Great Migration (1843), 7
Great Salt Lake, 13, 61–62
Great Sioux Reservation, 112
Green River, 5, 32, 44, 61, 78, 89
guard duties, 40–41, 51, 76

H
Hale, Israel F., 51, 53, 54
Hale, Titus, 51
Ham's Fork, 89

ABOUT THE AUTHOR

MARY BARMEYER O'BRIEN was born and raised in Missoula, Montana, and earned a B.A. in sociology from Linfield College (now Linfield University) in McMinnville, Oregon. She is the author of several previous books, both fiction and nonfiction, about women's history and pioneers on the overland trails, including *Heart of the Trail: Stories of Covered Wagon Women* and *The Promise of the West: Young Pioneers on the Overland Trails*. Mary writes from her home in the mountains of western Montana, where she and her husband, Dan, enjoy hiking, birdwatching, reading, and exploring.